First published in the UK 2022 by Sona Books
an imprint of Danann Media Publishing Ltd.

© 2022 Danann Media Publishing Limited

WARNING: For private domestic use only, any unauthorised Copying, hiring, lending or public performance of this book is illegal.

Published under licence from Future Publishing Limited a Future PLC group company. All rights reserved. No part of this publication may be reproduced or stored in a retrieval system or transmitted in any form or by any means without the prior written permission of the publisher.

© 2022 Future Publishing PLC

Copy Editor for Danann: Juliette O'Neill

Writing credits:
Grace Almond: p16; Michael E. Haskew: p48,82,110;
Joel McIver: p10,20,62,80,104,118,136; Henry Yates: p28,34,96,126

Picture credits:
Alamy: p2,6(t),8,11,12(t),13,16-18,19(l),20,25,26-30,36,48-51,53,60,65-67,71(r), 81,97-101,103,105(inset),111-117,122(bl),128-130,132,135,138;
Getty Images: p6,7,12,15,19,21,22,31-35,37-43,45-47,52,55-56,59,62-64,68-77,79-80, 82-87,89-90,93-95,104-109,115(t),118-127,130(m),131,136,139-140, Endpapers

CAT NO: SON0547
ISBN: 978-1-915343-07-9

Made in EU.

MAMA MIA!
HOW CAN I RESIST YOU?

They say the winner takes it all, and when it came to fame, fortune and writing their name into the annals of pop music, ABBA certainly did. But just how did four young Scandinavian singers join forces to become the biggest-selling pop band in history? Välkommen to the story of ABBA.

From their early days as budding artists to winning Eurovision, storming the global charts and bringing Australia to a hysterical halt, this is the history of arguably the most iconic pop act the world has ever seen.

With in-depth analysis of all nine studio albums, accounts from their tours and a look at how the band managed to keep turning out the smash hits even as their private lives collapsed, prepare to dive into a world of glitzy gear, record-breaking songs and blockbuster movies. Oh, and there's the fishy agreement that made it all possible. I hope you enjoy the journey. I do, I do, I do, I do, I do…

ABBA – Thank You For The Music

CONTENTS

8 — CHAPTER 1
KNOWING ME, KNOWING YOU

26 — CHAPTER 2
TAKE A CHANCE ON ME

60 — CHAPTER 3
MONEY, MONEY, MONEY

94 — CHAPTER 4
THANK YOU FOR THE MUSIC

108 — CHAPTER 5
MAMMA MIA!

124 — CHAPTER 6
A NEW VOYAGE

DISCOGRAPHY

- 24 — RING RING
- 44 — WATERLOO
- 54 — ABBA
- 58 — ARRIVAL
- 78 — ABBA: THE ALBUM
- 88 — VOULEZ-VOUS
- 92 — SUPER TROUPER
- 102 — THE VISITORS
- 134 — VOYAGE

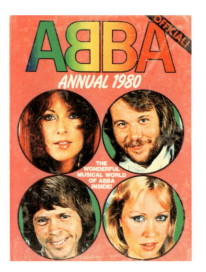

Contents

CHAPTER 1
KNOWING ME, KNOWING YOU

10 Just A Notion: The Origins Of ABBA

16 The Famous Foursome

20 Ring Ring: Superstardom Calling

24 Discography: Ring Ring

JUST A NOTION: THE ORIGINS OF ABBA

How Björn Ulvaeus and Benny Andersson became stars... even before ABBA

The roots of the biggest pure pop group of all time go back as far as World War II, but only just. On 25 April 1945, just four months before the world's superpowers agreed to co-exist in peace, a rather smaller – but still welcome – piece of good news was announced in the Swedish town of Gothenburg, when a baby called Björn Kristian Ulvaeus was born.

Around a year and a half later, Göran Bror Benny Andersson – as no one calls him – was born in Stockholm on 16 December 1946. Neither child had much in common, apart from both having younger sisters born in 1948, however both displayed a keen interest in music from an early age. Benny's father Gösta and grandfather Efraim both played the accordion, in line with the traditional Swedish music of the day, and presented him with his own instrument in early childhood. He later took up the piano.

It's interesting to note that the latter half of ABBA's career coincided with the rise of punk rock, perhaps their polar (pun intended) opposite in theme and sound. For this reason, when the Sex Pistols- and Clash-obsessed members of the press interviewed them in the late 1970s, the early folk-music leanings of Björn and Benny – and especially the latter's accordion skills – were the source of frequent derision. Perhaps slightly hurt by the mockery, Benny told the *NME:* "That is the popular traditional music of Northern Europe. Our folk songs sound like that. The first instrument I ever had was an accordion. My parents bought it for me when I was about ten."

To understand Björn and Benny's creative minds between becoming interested in music as kids and making it big with ABBA in 1974 – when they were the grand old age of 28 and 26 respectively – we need to understand what Swedish popular music really sounded like in the 1960s and early 1970s. Sure, American rock 'n' roll had made an impact on Swedish kids' lives, just as it had all over the world: the first single that Benny ever bought was Elvis

Right: Björn, of The Hootenanny Singers, and Benny, of The Hep Stars, writing songs together in 1970

Just A Notion: The Origins Of Abba

Presley's 'Jailhouse Rock', released in 1957 when he was just 11. Acoustic folk music co-existed with this new, more upbeat sound: however, Swedish folk – and specifically 'schlager', traditional-sounding songs with brass and other instrumentation – interested young people much more than the equivalent folk movement did in, say, the UK.

It wasn't long before both Björn and Benny joined bands that specialised in this feelgood, innocent sound. The former was a member of The Hootenanny Singers, whose name indicated their obvious interest in English-language music. Founded in 1961 when Björn was only 16 years old, the group also featured Johan Karlberg, Tonny Rooth and a German named Hansi Schwarz, and were astoundingly prolific: in the 1960s alone they released 21 singles, nine EPs and 11 studio and compilation albums. On top of this phenomenal work rate, the group toured incessantly and built a large domestic following, although they were barely known outside their home country.

In parallel, Benny found success as a keyboard player with another group, The Hep Stars, who he joined in 1964 and whose style owed a lot to The Beatles, from the haircuts on down. Founded in 1963, their best-known line-up was Benny plus vocalist Sven Hedlund, guitarist Jan Frisk, bassist Lennart Hegland and drummer Christer Pettersson. While enjoying the fruits of his success with The Hep Stars – whose recorded output was as popular, if not quite as sizeable, as that of The Hootenanny Singers – Benny also found time to marry his long-time girlfriend Christina Grönvall, with whom he had two children, Peter and Heléne. The marriage lasted until 1966, by which time Benny was a bona fide pop star.

As both bands enjoyed a heavy gigging schedule across Sweden, a meeting between the two future stars was

Opposite top: "It is writing songs, producing records and all that that's important to us. We have no ambitions to become big stars" – Björn and Benny, 1971. Global fame was just three years away

Opposite bottom: With Benny on the keyboard, The Hep Stars perform live on TV, January 1966

Björn visiting his hometown Västervik in southern Sweden, 1969

Benny Andersson in the studio with the group The Hep Stars 1967

Right: Björn and The Hootenanny Singers in Germany, January 1966

destined to occur sooner or later. As Björn later recalled, "I was touring with the Hootenanny Singers one summer – 1964, I think – and he was touring with the Hep Stars. We had 140 gigs over a period of three months and they had too, so we were bound to bump into each other, which we did, outside one of the gigs."

Yes, you read that correctly – a full year of touring for any normal band, compressed into three months. "We stopped the cars, got out and [said] 'What are you doing tonight?'" he continued. "As a matter of fact, the next day we, the three Hootenanny Singers, were going to start our military service, and so we were going to have a party in Linköping that night for our last day of freedom. So they said, 'Okay, we'll come and join you'. [They] turned up about 2 a.m. and the party was still going on. It ended with me and Benny sitting in the park playing guitars at dawn – most probably playing Beatles songs. There was an immediate rapport. I was the musical engine for my group and he was for his, [so] we had a lot of things in common. We stayed in touch and wrote songs off and on for the next few years."

After the mandatory year of military service ("Shooting and running about with helmets... so stupid!" sighed Björn), the two met up and began writing songs together. The first, 'Isn't It Easy To Say', was recorded by The Hep Stars, and the two writers continued to contribute songs to both bands' repertoires. In 1968, a hit came with 'Ljuva Sextiotal', for which the Hootenanny Singers' manager Stig Anderson wrote lyrics.

Talented though they were, the two musicians might never have ascended to the dizziest heights of pop stardom had it not been for two fortuitous meetings in 1969. The first came when Andersson attended an event on 1 March called the Melodifestivalen, where he encountered a brunette singer from Norway aged 23. The second occurred when a 19-year-old blonde from the town of Jönköping, already a well-known musician after a recent hit, bumped into Björn at the filming of a TV special in May.

Any guesses who these two singers were?

THE FAMOUS FOURSOME

ABBA's story began when a quartet of talented musicians decided to join forces and take the world by storm

Spanning a vibrant and successful decades-long career, the story of ABBA is as interesting and colourful as their music. Hailing from Sweden, ABBA (Agnetha Fältskog, Björn Ulvaeus, Benny Andersson and Anni-Frid Lyngstad) formed in Stockholm in 1972 and would later capture the imagination of millions around the globe, taking Swedish pop to the world stage. But how did Sweden's most successful musical group form?

Björn was born on 25 April 1945 in Gothenburg, Sweden, and took a keen interest in pursuing music at the age of 18, when he joined Swedish folk group The Hootenanny Singers as their frontman. Björn wrote some of the band's songs, including English-language tracks, and also released his own solo music.

Benny (born 16 December 1946) joined Swedish pop-rock group the Hep Stars aged 18 years old. The band, known as "the Swedish Beatles", performed covers of popular songs and Benny joined the group as their keyboardist and songwriter. Many of The Hep Stars' songs were

Left: Anni-Frid and Benny enjoy a meal at the Borsen restaurant in Stockholm, 1970

Right: Agnetha and Björn marry at Verum church in Verum, Sweden, 6 July 1971

hits in Sweden, including 'Sunny Girl', 'Wedding' and 'Consolation', which peaked at Number 1.

Like her fellow bandmates, Anni-Frid Lyngstad, born on 15 November 1945 in Bjørkåsen, Ballangen, Norway, fell in love with music from an early age. Aged just 13, she sang with various dance bands and formed her own band, the Anni-Frid Four. After winning a national talent competition and the prize of a recording contract with EMI Sweden, she released several singles on the label but was unable to achieve success with her solo music.

Björn in his parent's living room in 1972. On his left is his father Gunnar and mother Aina

Final band member Agnetha Fältskog (born 5 April 1950 in Jönköping, Sweden) received early praise from Karl-Gerhard Lundkvist, a Swedish rocker who heard her sing on the track 'Jag var så kär' (I Was So In Love) and scouted her, inviting her to Stockholm to record her songs. Similarly, to Benny and Björn, she found herself entering the music industry at the age of 18 with a Number 1 record. Agnetha also recorded covers of popular songs from around the world and released four solo LPs between 1968 and 1971.

ABBA's story began in Stockholm, Sweden, where Björn and Benny met in June 1966. Benny and Björn would occasionally meet when their bands were on tour, but it was in June 1966 that they decided to attempt to write their first song together, 'Isn't It Easy to Say'. The song was later recorded by Benny's band, The Hep Stars. After meeting Stig Anderson, Hootenanny Singers' manager and founder of the record label, Polar Music, Benny and Björn were encouraged to continue writing songs together.

Benny's song 'Hej, Clown' ranked second place at Melodifestivalen in 1969, the festival that selects the Swedish entry to the Eurovision Song Contest. It was here that he met his future wife and fellow ABBA member Anni-Frid Lyngstad.

A few weeks later, they met in southern Sweden and became a couple, with Benny producing Anni-Frid's single 'Peter Pan' in September 1969. Benny also produced her debut album, *Frida*. Notably, the album also included the original Swedish rendition of the hit ABBA song 'Fernando'. While Anni-Frid had struggled to achieve chart success with her earlier solo work, her single 'Min egen stad' (My Own Town), produced by Benny, reached Number 1.

In 1970, Benny and Björn recorded their first album together, *Lycka* (Happiness), and were occasionally joined by their partners for the recording process, who added their backing vocals to the album. The following year, Björn and Agnetha married, and, in 1972, Agnetha starred in the original Swedish production of *Jesus Christ Superstar* as Mary Magdalene.

Their first collaboration as a group occurred in the most heart-warming, natural way, when the two couples went on holiday to Cyprus: after singing for fun, they gave an improvised live performance to United Nations soldiers stationed on the island. It was around this time that Benny and Björn were recording *Lycka*, and, after Agnetha and Anni-Frid added their backing vocals to the album, the group floated the idea of launching their act, Festfolket (Party People).

18-year-old Anni-Frid Lyngstad at her home in Eskilstuna, Sweden, 1964

Studio portrait of Agnetha Fältskog, 1968

Festfolket was envisioned as a cabaret show lasting approximately 45 minutes, featuring live musical performances and comedy skits, and included various songs from their individual careers, as well as some songs that had been written specially for the show. After two months of rehearsals, Festfolket opened on 1 November 1970 at a restaurant in Gothenburg called Trägår'n. It then changed venues, moving to the Strand Cabaret in Stockholm a month later, with a minor tour in Sweden in the spring of 1971.

Interestingly, considering the success they would go on to achieve as ABBA, Festfolket garnered rather negative reviews: this was the first time Anni-Frid, Benny, Björn and Agnetha had collaborated officially as a group on stage, and, reportedly, audience members showed little interest in their show, although their performance of 'Hej, gamle man' received some praise.

This rather infamous chapter in the group's history led them to postpone future plans to collaborate and decide to concentrate on their solo projects again. Subsequent interviews have seen the group reminisce about the show, with Björn remarking in an interview in May 2013 that it was "the low end of the collaboration between the four of us". He continued, calling it "embarrassing". Separately, Agnetha said, "It was not a success, generally comprising of a thin spread of vapid jokes and other people's songs."

However, they did release their first official record together, 'Hej, gamle man' (Hey, Old Man), which reached Number 5 on the sales charts and Number 1 on the Svensktoppen (the weekly records chart airing on Sveriges Radio). They began to contribute more to each other's solo work, providing backing vocals, instrumentation and production, as well as song writing. Agnetha, Benny and Björn toured together in May 1971, with Anni-Frid touring on her own. Later recording sessions would see the foursome collaborate even more.

ABBA's earlier years were the band's chance to find their sound and learn to work collaboratively. While Festfolket didn't gain the traction they wanted, they laid the foundation for their future success, groundwork that would see them go on to become the biggest pop group in not just Swedish but international history. For that reason alone the group will forever hold a special place in the annals of pop.

RING RING SUPERSTARDOM CALLING

How an unforgettable melody launched four stratospheric careers

A heavily pregnant Agnetha performs 'Ring Ring'

ow that Björn and Agnetha and Benny and Anni-Frid were couples, presumably the stage was set for the group to take flight and achieve instant stardom – correct?

Well, not exactly. The journey from their individual first meetings around 1969 to actual bona fide stardom lasted a gruelling five years – and don't forget, three of the four musicians were no longer teenagers at this stage. By 1970, when the soon-to-be pop foursome's careers were still a long way over the horizon, three of them were aged 24 or older: the temptation to bow to the pressure of conservative Sweden and begin a 'real' career must have been significant. Only Fältskog, a wide-eyed 19 years old as the group convened at the beginning of the new decade, was of the age we usually associate with pop starlets.

It's just as well, then, that the new band – still unnamed at this stage – hit the ground running, with the two men writing an album, *Lycka*, and asking Agnetha and Anni-Frid to add backing vocals. Yet the foursome had still not

Performing together on the ZDF Music Show: DISCO, 1973

committed to working together in the long term at this point, with Agnetha, Benny and Björn touring together and Anni-Frid playing shows as a solo artist.

More Björn & Benny-released songs were written for Sweden's Melodifestivalen in 1971 and 1972, leading to some domestic recognition when 'Säg det med en sång' (Say It with A Song) became a hit. Three subsequent singles were released in Japan in 1972, and the group also saw minor success in the U.S. – under the snappy name Björn & Benny, Agnetha & Anni-Frid – with 'People Need Love'.

However, it was the single 'Ring Ring' which first hinted at the expansive sound that would make its creators into stars. A superficially slight song about waiting for a lover to call, the song had bigger dimensions than earlier releases thanks to a 'wall of sound' production influenced heavily by the work of the American studio guru Phil Spector. The song only came third in Melodifestivalen in 1973 – and didn't qualify for Eurovision entry as a result – but much greater success greeted it throughout mainland Europe, and it topped the charts in Sweden in two versions, the original and an English-language version with lyrics translated by none other than the American singer Neil Sedaka.

The song was helped along immeasurably by manager Stig Anderson's decision to rename the quartet (more on that later), and the *Ring Ring* album, which led off with its title track, charted highly in Belgium, the Netherlands, Norway and South Africa. Stig Anderson was bent on a hit in the UK and U.S., however: his objective was to achieve an English-language hit for the newly renamed band that would provide truly global stardom. Having come close to Eurovision success before, he remained convinced the contest was ABBA's best route to global fame. The mission was clear: roll on 1974...

Stig Anderson helped pen 'Ring Ring' and went on to manage the band for many years

"IT'S KIND OF A MIRACLE. NEVER IN OUR WILDEST DREAMS DID WE THINK THAT THESE SONGS WE WROTE WOULD LAST SO LONG"

BENNY ANDERSSON
ON ABBA'S INCREDIBLE LONGEVITY

RING RING

On their debut album, ABBA took a few creative wrong turns but also showcased the songs and the sound that would later catapult them to greatness

Drop the needle onto side one of this debut album and the most noticeable aspect is that much of it sounds nothing like ABBA. This is hardly surprising though, as this is a document of a band in the process of forging its own sound. Following the 1972 success of the single 'People Need Love' by the band then known as Björn, Benny, Agnetha and Anni-Frid, the group's manager Stig Anderson decided the quartet needed to record an album.

Ring Ring
RELEASED 26 March 1973
TRACKLIST

SIDE A
1. Ring Ring
2. Another Town, Another Train
3. Disillusion
4. People Need Love
5. I Saw It In The Mirror
6. Nina, Pretty Ballerina

SIDE B
1. Love Isn't Easy (But It Sure Is Hard Enough)
2. Me And Bobby And Bobby's Brother
3. He Is Your Brother
4. Ring Ring (English)
5. I Am Just A Girl
6. Rock 'N' Roll Band

The result is a mixed bag. Second track 'Another Town, Another Train' features Björn on lead vocals. It's a solid composition, but in the context of 1973 it sounds woefully dated. Saccharine production, copious dollops of flute and lyrics such as 'You and I had a groovy time' make it feel like a sonic hangover from the late-'60s. 'I Saw It In The Mirror', featuring lead vocals by Björn and Benny, is similarly lacking, despite its lush electric piano, tasteful bass and sparse production. In his book *ABBA: Let The Music Speak* author Chris Patrick describes the track as an "uninspired attempt at laidback R&B".

All four members share lead vocals on 'Love Isn't Easy', which hurtles stylistically between LA singer-songwriter balladry and novelty pop, with fleeting hard rock and country rock flourishes in between. It's a cloying mish-mash of a song and arguably the album's real low point.

By complete contrast, *Ring Ring* contains some real high points, and the most notable of these is the title track, which opens the album. Like all great pop songs, it's a simple structure with a strong, infectious chorus and features glam-rock elements prevalent at the time. Written by Björn, Benny and manager Stig, the song came third in the 1973 Melodifestivalen and the English version features lyrics contributed by Neil Sedaka and his writing partner Phil Cody.

The track reached Number 1 in Sweden and gave the band their first major break in numerous European countries. It also showcased the beginnings of the sound that would come to define ABBA. The track was recorded on 10 January 1973 at Metronome Studio in Stockholm with engineer Michael B. Tretow, who would go on to engineer and produce numerous albums and singles by ABBA and have a defining impact on their unique sound.

Discography: Ring Ring

At the time of recording *Ring Ring*, Tretow had been reading a biography about producer Phil Spector, renowned for his 'wall of sound'. Spector had achieved this impressive sonic impact by having several musicians playing the same instruments at the same time. This technique was too costly for *Ring Ring*, so Tretow's solution was to simply record the backing track twice and meld them together to create a massive orchestral sound.

Tretow also changed the speed of the tape between the overdubs, making the instruments marginally out of tune, which increased the effect. Nothing like this had ever been done before in Swedish music. On the *Ring Ring* track, which featured Anni-Frid and Agnetha on lead vocals, Tretow's sonic ingenuity brought a whole new dynamism and impact to the band's sound.

The album was strengthened further by the addition of the band's 1972 debut single *People Need Love*, a strong pop stomper that also benefited from Tretow's Spector-style experimentation.

Another of the album's highlights was 'Disillusion', a powerful and emotive piano ballad, sung by Agnetha and written by her and Björn. When Anni-Frid enters the mix on harmonies, the stirrings of the trademark ABBA vocal sound really come to the fore.

As an album, *Ring Ring* is certainly fitful and erratic at times. But it contains some real standout moments. Despite taking some creative wrong turns while striving to achieve their unique voice, it is the sound of a band on the brink of greatness, an involving and invaluable work.

CHAPTER 2
TAKE A CHANCE ON ME

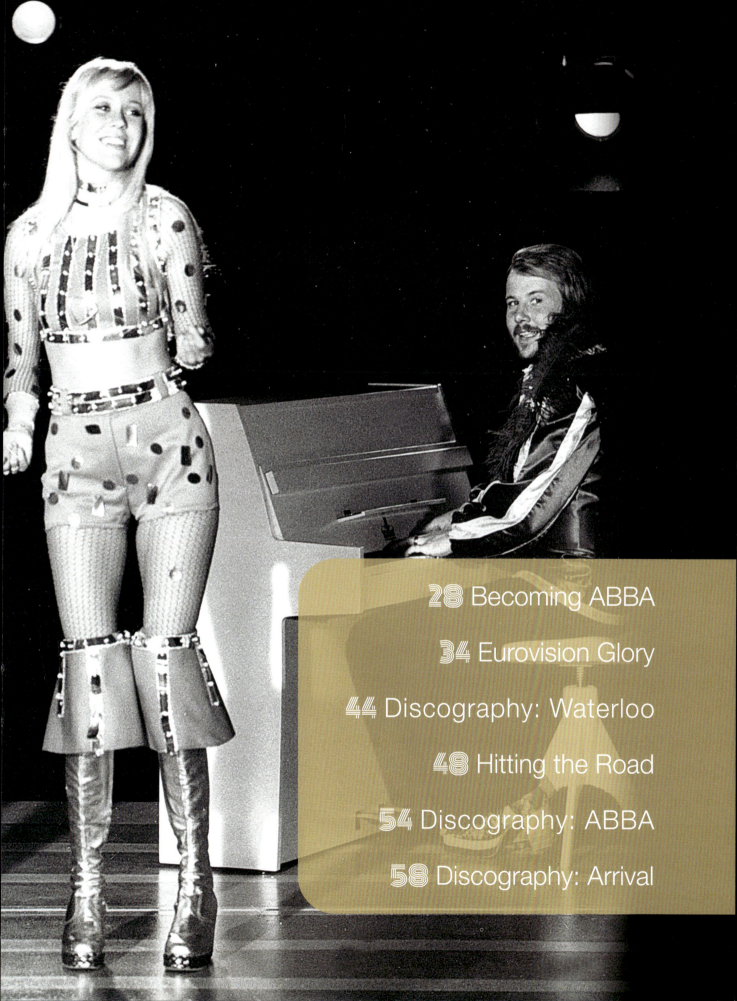

28 Becoming ABBA

34 Eurovision Glory

44 Discography: Waterloo

48 Hitting the Road

54 Discography: ABBA

58 Discography: Arrival

BECOMING ABBA

The birth of ABBA was a branding masterclass from pop's sharpest brain. From the band name to the logo, this is how four Scandinavians became a sensation

The four members were assembled and the musical chemistry undeniable. But in the early '70s, a thousand more variables stood between the soon-to-be ABBA and pop greatness – and none of them would have aligned without Stig Anderson.

Too often, the band's late manager and svengali is reduced to a footnote. Yet it was Anderson's entrepreneurial drive – hard-won through his childhood poverty and scramble up the slippery pole of showbiz – that thrust his charges into global contention. Not just a tack-sharp business brain and prolific song publisher (whose firms included Sweden Music and Polar Music) but a creative talent in his own right (with lyrical contributions that took in 'Dancing Queen' and 'S.O.S'), Anderson was a hot-tempered cyclone of hyperactivity, spinning however many plates it took.

"He was on the phone all the time," Anderson's then-teenage daughter Marie told *The Daily Telegraph* in 2018. "This was before telex and the internet. He was always speaking to America, Japan, Australia…"

The most pressing priority, considered the canny Anderson, was a band name that would cross oceans, burst through language barriers and trip off the tongue in such target markets as the UK and America. By those criteria, the quartet's current billing as Björn & Benny, Agnetha & Anni-Frid was a non-starter. Terminally cumbersome, overloaded with syllables, umlauts and ugly punctuation, the name was too long for magazine covers and a stumbling block for radio DJs.

Four Christian names was plainly too much of a mouthful. But perhaps there was something that could be done with those mirror-image initials. For some time, Anderson had doodled the four letters onto internal paperwork – A, B, B, A – to gain the attention of Agnetha, Björn, Benny and Anni-Frid. He had even started using the acronym in conversations with the national media.

"The newspapers here in Scandinavia called me, very often at that time," reflected Anderson in an Australian video interview, "and I became just fed up every time having to say, 'I'm speaking about Björn, Benny, Agnetha and Frida'. So I sat down and thought for a couple of days. And I started to call them ABBA. It was quite natural for me."

Informally, the music press quickly took Anderson up on the nickname, even if the members themselves resisted. "Our name is not ABBA, nor has it ever been," Björn testily

The world was their oyster: a beaming Benny and Anni-Frid would marry, divorce and taste global stardom

told an interviewer in the spring of 1973. "The newspapers call us that, we ourselves don't."

Aware that the customer is always right, Anderson decided to put out the feelers. In an age before social media, asking for fan input was a novel concept, and although a poll taken by the Swedish media saw the public offer up alternatives (Baba, Alibaba and Friends And Neighbours being the least-worst entries), the manager's instincts were confirmed. "We had one of the biggest newspapers here in Sweden ask the youngsters, 'What would you like to call this group?'" he recalled. "And of course, they already had heard about ABBA at that time, so I think 90 per cent of them said ABBA."

Yet there was still a sticking point, with Anderson well aware of the Swedish canned fish company who had laid claim to the ABBA moniker first. "Our name was a joke," he told the same Australian interviewer, "simply because ABBA is a very well-known manufacturer here of herrings. So it sounded a little bit ridiculous to start with."

In fact, Anderson was deadly serious, writing to the canning firm's management and requesting shared ownership of the ABBA name. "And they wrote back," the band reflected in *The Guardian*, "and said it was fine as long as we didn't do anything that reflected badly on the fish industry."

Agnetha and Björn with their newborn daughter Linda, February 1973

Even then, Benny would put up tongue-in-cheek resistance, complaining that the band "would now smell of canned fish". But in the absence of a better option, ABBA it was. "I think the first time we used it was in Brighton, when we won the Eurovision Song Contest there [in 1974]," recalled Anderson. "That was the very first time we used just the name ABBA."

As it turned out, that band name came with a secret weapon that not even Anderson had foreseen. That same year of 1974, ABBA's first releases shipped in non-descript sleeves, with their new billing rendered in a cartoonish font that was anonymous at best. Two years later, it was the designer Rune Söderqvist who spotted the weak link in this precision-tooled pop juggernaut, pointing out to ABBA photographer and friend Ola Lager that the band's current logo was "awful". Lager passed the criticism up the chain of command – and Anderson duly challenged Söderqvist to submit something better.

The music industry of the mid-'70s was a time of excess in all things – music, money, drugs – and that extended to band logos. With the Rolling Stones setting the bar at the

THE FUNKY FOUR

ANNI-FRID LYNGSTAD

Lyngstad's unmistakable mezzo-soprano voice was one of the greatest weapons in ABBA's armoury: a head-turning sound that could either lock seamlessly with that of Agnetha or soar solo on anthems like 'Fernando'. Anni-Frid rolled with the punches of her divorce from Benny, and as she flew out of the blocks post-ABBA with 1982's Phil Collins-produced solo album, *Something's Going On*, she briefly looked set to be the band's breakaway success story.

However, after 1984's slower-selling *Shine*, her output become more sporadic and low-key: when she made a guest appearance on guitarist Jojje Wadenius' 2010 album *Reconnection*, it had been a full six years since her last appearance in a studio. As such, Björn was "prepared" for Anni-Frid to refuse the reunion – but *Voyage* wouldn't have been the same without her.

BJÖRN ULVAEUS

As far back as he can remember, Björn told *The Guardian* in 2020, he felt a "pressure to achieve". Perhaps that explains the guitarist's unbeatable strike-rate as the counterpoint of ABBA's writing partnership – not to mention his enduring role in selling ABBA to the world as the band's unofficial spokesman (even today, Björn grants vastly more interviews than any other member).

Witty, erudite and renowned for his ability to transform Benny's material with a twist of his own genius, Björn co-wrote the soundtrack to the 1970s, and despite his divorce from Agnetha at that decade's end, he appears to have come through the meat grinder of fame with his heart still open. "I suspect my favourite word could be love," he confessed in that same *Guardian* interview, "despite its drawbacks in the rhyming department."

dawn of the decade with their enduring 'lips' motif, a scan of the record store shelves revealed designs spanning from Aerosmith's winged calling card to KISS's lightning bolt-styled typeface. The ABBA logo pitched by Söderqvist could not have been further removed from those opulent schoolboy doodles. A masterstroke of clean and utilitarian Scandi design, it was little more than four letters in a News Gothic-style font. The genius twist was the reversal of the first 'B': a simple switch-up that both evoked the internal dynamics of ABBA – two couples working in unity – and offered a flash of symmetry that was instantly magnetic to buyers.

Any music industry professional will bear witness that all the planets have to align for a pop band to ascend to greatness. But when ABBA's *Arrival* album debuted in October 1976 – fronted by Söderqvist's eye-catching logo and with a tracklisting that included the immortal 'Dancing Queen', 'Knowing Me, Knowing You' and 'Money, Money, Money' – it was the perfect storm and the culmination of everything that Anderson and his cohorts had strived for. Even the title of that breakthrough album was apt indeed. Now fully formed in every way, ABBA had arrived.

Power pose: a young Anni-Frid during a visit to the U.S.

BENNY ANDERSSON

ABBA's songwriting partnership is unthinkable without Benny Andersson, whom Björn once referred to as the "musical motor, providing most of the music, even in the early days". A prolific self-taught multi-instrumentalist, Benny was able to dart between guitar, keyboards and even accordion – though not vocals, which he never contributed again after 1974's 'Suzy-Hang-Around' – and even when ABBA's personal relationships turned sour in the late '70s, his melodic instincts never faltered.

In modern times, ruffle-haired, twinky-eyed and avuncular – not to mention free of the drink problems that dogged his early years of stardom – he most resembles a benevolent mad professor and still visits his Stockholm studio every day to tinker with works in progress. Don't bet against Benny writing a few more classics before he's done.

AGNETHA FÄLTSKOG

"I am the girl with golden hair," she sang in 1978's 'Thank You For The Music', and among ABBA's more superficial fans, the line summed up Agnetha's status as the Swedish group's eye candy. Certainly, set against the greys and browns of 1970s Britain, the singer's Scandinavian beauty-in-excelsis was a focal point. But as Agnetha once firmly reminded a journalist, "I'm not only a nice bottom". Far from it as a matter of fact.

The power and emotion of her coloratura soprano voice was astonishing, while her interpretative gifts both deepened the work of Björn and Benny and elevated the group as whole. When Agnetha sang 'The Winner Takes It All' in the wake of her divorce from its author, the words seemed to come not from a lyric sheet but a deep well of sorrow within: it was perhaps her finest hour.

Björn, Agnetha, Anni-Frid and Benny give the camera a thumbs up after winning Eurovision 1974 in Brighton

ABBA – Thank You For The Music

EUROVISION
GLORY

One night in April 1974, a fateful performance of 'Waterloo' turned a Scandi pop curio into a global sensation. This is the story of ABBA's lift-off…

Eurovision Glory

The winners with song writer and manager Stig Anderson and conductor Sven-Olof Walldoff

For almost half a century, the history books on the shelf have preserved ABBA in aspic as the poster children of the Eurovision Song Contest. At the event's 50th anniversary in 2005, the Swedish band's winning entry of 1974 – 'Waterloo' – was crowned the greatest song of them all. Fast-forward to 2020 and a major BBC viewers poll once again propelled the anthem to the top spot. At last year's singing competition in Rotterdam, a 14-country open vote put the consensus beyond all doubt. Waterloo is, quite simply, the one. What else?

What fewer people know is that ABBA's first brushes with the continent's flagship music contest were bruising failures. As early as 1969, while still toiling as backroom songwriters for hire, Björn Ulvaeus and Benny Andersson had submitted their cabaret-style singalong, 'Ljuva Sextital', only to see it stall at the Melodifestivalen national heat stages.

That same year, Anni-Frid Lyngstad also performed 'Härlig är Vår Jord' (Glorious Is Our Earth) and earned a humble fourth place for her troubles.

"It makes me realise why and how music sometimes becomes consumer goods," she reflected on Swedish Radio in 2004. "But it was an exciting and incredibly nervous experience."

Undeterred, in 1972, Björn and Benny hunkered down with three other songwriters (Stig Anderson, Wayne Bickerton and Tony Waddington) to gift Swedish singer Lena Andersson with the wistful 'Säj Det Med En Sang' (Better To Have Loved). The bitter-sweet trill and rousing orchestration was a signpost to the genius that lay ahead, but once again the song failed to advance beyond the Swedish borders.

Even when the ABBA lineup fronted their own first entry in 1973, Björn, Benny, Anni-Frid and Agnetha Fältskog fared little better, with future classic 'Ring Ring' suffering the humiliation of limping in as runner-up to Nova & The Dolls' eminently forgettable 'Sommar'n Som Aldrig Säger Nej'.

"The straight translation into English would be Your Breasts Are Like Nesting Swallows," sighed a despairing Björn in a *Billboard* interview years later. "There was an uproar in the papers from people writing in, 'How could you choose the wrong song?' It was so evident, and 'Ring Ring' became a huge hit and the other one just a minor hit. But we [still] had tremendous self-confidence

Swedish newspaper Expressen announces ABBA's win with the headline "What a party!"

ABBA at the 1974 Eurovision Song Contest, which was held in Brighton, England

because of the huge hit we had with 'Ring Ring' all over Scandinavia and Holland and Belgium. And we weren't discouraged, because we knew they were going to change the jury system."

"We were much more glam rock in '73 – we were all sequins, all four of us," Benny reflected in 2008. He added sniffily, "We didn't win because they had this jury that consisted of music people. Journalists. Experts."

Even then, smarting from rejection, the Swedes still recognised that the Eurovision Song Contest – beamed to millions of households across the continent, and not yet the tongue-in-cheek kitsch-fest it would later become – was the shop window they needed to escape the domestic market and make ABBA a full-time project.

"That was the dream from early on," Björn told *Mojo*'s Jim Irvin in 1999. "We had a hit in Japan in about 1972, a big hit, with 'People Move On': that was the first taste of what it could be, and it was a minor hit in Holland. But it was very, very difficult to get people in England and America to even listen to a group from Sweden, virtually impossible."

Conceptually, too, Eurovision was the perfect fit, with Björn telling *The Guardian* that "ABBA was such a European idea. We took our inspiration from French chansons, German schlager, Italian ballads and Nordic folk."

Eurovision qualifying – 1970s style

ABBA – Thank You For The Music

Taking in the sights of Brighton, 1974

And so, at the tail-end of 1973, ABBA dusted themselves down, rallied and readied a new song for the following year's Melodifestivalen. But events could have played out very differently. Until late in the process, the band had pegged the lesser-known 'Hasta Mañana' – sung solo by Agnetha – as their best hope. "Which is a good song," reflected Andersson in the Netflix documentary *This Is Pop*. "But we said, 'No, we should have something that would represent what we want to do', not necessarily adjust to what they might like at the Eurovision, which is more of a European traditional schlager."

As Björn has since reflected, "'Hasta Mañana' would never have won and all this would never have happened". Better, he considered, to submit a "riskier" song that was "much more fun to perform".

That song could only be 'Waterloo'. Penned, as ever, by Björn and Benny, it was an instant classic built on pounding piano and call-and-response vocals that once again owed a palpable debt to glam-rock (and especially the 1973 Wizzard tune 'See My Baby Jive').

'Waterloo's multiple overdubs were inspired by producer Phil Spector's epic 'wall of sound' approach, while the lyric (originally sung in Swedish by Agnetha and Anni-Frid) drew unlikely parallels between a woman surrendering to a man's advances and the 1815 routing of Napoleon Bonaparte's armies by the British-led Seventh Coalition. "Stig rightly suggested that the song should have an international theme," Björn told the British journalist Pete Paphides, "so we all came up with Waterloo." Not that ABBA were necessarily referencing the famous skirmish. "Waterloo is a pop song about someone meeting their own Waterloo," the band would later clarify. "It is not about the battle."

Whatever the 'Waterloo' lyric's motivations, it has since been held up as ABBA's wordsmanship at its sharpest. "'Waterloo' on first hearing can easily be written off as typical Abbian popsy-wopsian hokum," wrote journalist Joe Queenan in *The Guardian*'s Vinyl Word series. "But a closer examination of the lyrics reveals the band's astonishingly deft insights into the nuances of 19th-century European geopolitics and also demonstrates the quartet's remarkable ability to re-contextualise the lessons of that dark period for our own times."

Even with its history of backing the wrong horse, the 1974 Melodifestivalen could not fail to see 'Waterloo' for the stone-cold pop classic it would soon become. On 9 February, ABBA's new song was put before the Swedish public for consideration and stole an almost unanimous victory to be nodded through as the national entry. And so to Eurovision.

Eurovision Glory

With back-to-back winner Luxembourg passing up its right to host the event for a second consecutive year on the grounds of expense, the 1974 contest was to take place at the UK's grand Brighton Dome, built at the British seaside resort for the Prince Regent in 1803. Seventeen countries would compete, with Greece making its debut and France dropping out as a mark of respect following the death of President Georges Pompidou.

As was Eurovision tradition, the entrants were mostly obscure, old-fashioned or arcane. To modern audiences, their names and faces now mean little: it's unlikely that Yugoslavian rockers Korni Grupa or Israel's long-defunct Poogy exist beyond the realms of the toughest pub quizzes.

The notable exception was soon-to-be Grease star Olivia Newton-John, representing the UK with 'Long Live Love': a twee singalong she secretly hated. "Once a week you'd sing on TV and people would write in and vote for the one they wanted," reflected the singer in one interview. "So the people voted this one. Then I had to go sing it for the country, not liking it, which wasn't easy."

Meanwhile, from across the Baltic Sea came the Swedish hot-tips, billed by Eurovision's TV commentator as 'the ABBA group'. "We changed into our stage outfits at the hotel," Björn recalled in *Billboard* of preparations for the show on 6 April, "and a bus came to take us to the arena. I was overweight and couldn't sit down because my trousers would split."

Eight songs into an unspectacular competition, all eyes were suddenly on ABBA. Following a bizarre lead-in from producer Sven-Olof Walldoff in full Napoleon costume, the band burst onto the stage and into pop culture, wearing eye-catching costumes that included Björn's shuriken-shaped guitar and stacked-heel silver boots. "They enter Eurovision singing about the Battle of Waterloo in platforms," reflected Oasis leader and unlikely ABBA fan Noel Gallagher in 2004. "Fucking come on, all shagging each other? Get in, does it get better than that?"

Performing 'Waterloo' at the Melodifestivalen

"My grandson couldn't believe that the chubby guy with the star-shaped guitar was me," reflected a seventy-something Björn in a video message before the 2020 contest. "He looked incredulous. And to tell you the truth, when I watch that clip from the Eurovision Song Contest in Brighton, I find it very hard to believe as well. But then, the ESC is one hell of a launching pad."

No kidding. Having ripped through 'Waterloo' in slightly halting English (by happy chance, the rule that required entrants to sing in their native tongue was dropped in 1974), ABBA became the night's runaway winners. By the time the dust settled, the Swedish entry had racked up a total of 24 points, easily beating closest contenders Italy (Gigliola Cinquetti's 'Si', with 18 points), and the Netherlands (Mouth & MacNeal's 'I See A Star', with 15 points). As for Newton-John's 'Long Live Love', that came in fourth place, with 14 points.

"Well, actually I had a £20 bet on it, in Brighton, at 20/1," Benny told the Music Business Worldwide site of the triumphant moment. "There were some good songs, but I did think that ours was better. I was standing there, and I'm good at mental arithmetic, so I knew exactly the moment where we would win even if we got no more votes, and I told the others, 'That's it, we've done it'."

Following the victory, and appropriately enough, the band spent the night partying at the Napoleon Suite of the Grand Brighton Hotel. "I think the best memory was afterwards, when I finally got to bed at three o'clock in the morning," reflected Björn to Eurovision TV. "And I realised that we had gone from being a fairly unknown group in Sweden to a group that everyone had seen. The world was open to us, just overnight, and when that dawned on me, that was the most fantastic experience."

Without 'Waterloo' and Eurovision, ABBA might have remained a cult concern in a cultural backwater; portfolio musicians spinning endless plates just to stay solvent. But

Enjoying some beach time on Brighton's pebbled shore after the contest

The band's success lives on in Brighton at the Sand Sculpture Festival with the theme Music in Sand

with that performance to light the touchpaper, their entire outlook and trajectory changed.

"Before that," Björn told Sky News, "Benny and I had been in a rat race. We were running around producing other people's records, writing songs for other people, even going on tours in different constellations just to pay the rent. From 'Waterloo' onward, when the royalties came pouring in, we could afford to say 'no' to everything else and just concentrate on the writing. That's when you get better at it. And that's what I wish for most songwriters today."

Notoriously, the UK's Eurovision panel didn't cast a single vote for Sweden. But it seemed the British public knew better. The studio version of 'Waterloo' had been recorded the previous December at Metronome Studio with regular ABBA contributors Janne Schaffer, Rutger Gunnarsson and Ola Brunkert. Now, with the 'Waterloo' single already pressed and shipping across Europe, the song raced up the charts to become the band's first UK#1. "The Brits were the first ones to embrace us after winning," Björn told BBC Breakfast in 2021. "Kind of strange they would give us zero points. It sounds like they were trying to do something cunning."

Meanwhile, the band's projection of the perks of a Eurovision win were vindicated. 'Waterloo' topped the charts in Belgium, Denmark, Finland, West Germany, Ireland, Norway and Switzerland, while scaling the Top 3 in Austria, France, Holland and Spain.

The song would doubtless have hit #1 on the band's home turf of Sweden, too, had a quirk of the country's charting system not meant that singles and albums appeared in the same rundown, leading to 'Waterloo' (the song) being held off the top spot by *Waterloo* (the album, also released that year). "There's never such a thing as a guaranteed success, never," Björn told *The Liverpool Echo*. "No one knows. I've experienced that so often in my life, that people think it's a no-brainer."

But Europe was just the start. Marching onward, the 'Waterloo' single also broke into the Top 10 of such untapped but highly lucrative markets as Australia, South Africa, Canada, New Zealand, Rhodesia and critically, the US, whose customary coolness towards the Swedes warmed a little. "Just when the Top 40 was plumbing hitherto-unfathomable, moribund depths, along came their single, 'Waterloo'," wrote Ken Barnes in his *Rolling Stone* review. "A modern-day 'girl group' production with the brightest, most exuberant sound around, it's made button-punching on the car radio a worthwhile pastime again."

Even so, the popular narrative of an overnight success doesn't quite square with what happened next. Curiously, in the wake of 'Waterloo', and with the pop industry's jugular exposed, ABBA released a run of tanking singles that saw their stock plummet. 'Honey, Honey', the aforementioned 'Hasta Mañana', the limp 'So Long', the long-forgotten 'I've Been Waiting For You':

all non-charting misfires in the UK that did much to sap the band's briefly rocketing momentum.

"It was a very difficult period," Björn admitted to *Billboard*. "We thought we should release something that was more rock 'n' roll. 'So Long' was more in the vein of Sweet and Mud and all those groups. That was a mistake. But everyone had decided we were a one-hit wonder because we came from Eurovision. And, with very few exceptions, they are one-hit wonders. So that helped, especially in the UK, to hold us back."

"After we won the Eurovision Song Contest and had a big hit with 'Waterloo' all over the world," picked up Benny in an interview with SBS, "then nothing happened, like often is the way with Eurovision Song Contest contenders. So from sending us big limousines in the 'Waterloo' period, the cars got smaller and smaller and we had a Volkswagen bus by the end!"

Maybe so – but the bigger-picture impact of Eurovision on ABBA's career cannot be understated. 'Waterloo' represented far more than one night of fleeting glory or an isolated smash-hit single. When ABBA regrouped and once again struck gold with the perfect song (1975's 'S.O.S'), the groundwork laid by Eurovision ensured they had the platform and profile to fly. And from that moment on, the '70s were theirs for the taking.

Womble Uncle Bulgaria joins the fab four at the Eurovision Song Contest

WATERLOO

Blistering success at the Eurovision Song Contest would propel the band forward for their second studio album

On the evening of Saturday 6 April 1974, Swedish record producer, composer and conductor Sven-Olof Walldoff marched briskly towards the orchestra podium at Brighton Dome dressed as Napoleon Bonaparte. It was a witty gesture and a fitting premise to the joyous, soaring performance that was to follow.

Walldoff was there to conduct the orchestra on the ABBA song 'Waterloo', Sweden's entry for the Eurovision Song Contest that year. Seconds later, as Benny, Björn and session musicians Rutger Gunnarsson (bass) and Ola Brunkert (drums) launched into the opening bars of the song, Anni-Frid and Agnetha bounded out onto the stage area to deliver a performance that would become seared into the public's consciousness for ever.

Benny, Björn and manager Stig Anderson had succeeded in writing a killer song – a soaring, joyful, thunderously paced composition with an unforgettable chorus. Released as the first single from the second studio album of the same name, it topped the charts in the UK and numerous European countries.

The song showcased the sonic template that would come to define Abba: thick vocal harmonies, powerful production, multiple overdubs and strident piano. Despite the success of the 'Waterloo' song, this album is very much the sound of a band in transition, yet to fully embrace the style and sound for which it would be known.

What is surprising is how prominent Björn and Benny's voices still are on this release. Equally surprising are the wildly diverse styles at play here. 'Sitting In The Palmtree', the second track, is built around a sparse, lilting reggae groove. It has a sound that is arguably ahead of its time, although the lyrics defy belief: 'People laugh and point their fingers / Like I was a monkey at the zoo,' intones Björn at one point. More baffling is 'What About Livingstone', which has all the traits of a novelty song, complete with Frida's vocal being processed to sound like she has ingested helium.

'King Kong Song' – which features lead vocals by Björn, Agnetha and Anni-Frid – lurches into life with heavy rock guitar riffage and pounding piano. It's reminiscent of a stage musical such as *The Rocky Horror Show*, complete with '50s rock 'n' roll references. But lyrically, it's a non-starter: 'What a dreadful mighty killer / A big black wild gorilla'.

ABBA: The Album
RELEASED 4 March 1974
TRACKLIST

SIDE A
1. Waterloo
2. Sitting In The Palmtree
3. King Kong Song
4. Hasta Mañana
5. My Mama Said
6. Dance (While The Music Still Goes On)

SIDE B
1. Honey, Honey
2. Watch Out
3. What About Livingstone?
4. Gonna Sing You My Lovesong
5. Suzy-Hang-Around

Discography: Waterloo

After 'Waterloo', 'Honey Honey' – the second single from the album, sung by Agnetha and Frida – is probably the next most familiar song on the album, thanks largely to its inclusion in the *Mamma Mia!* musical. The likeable folk pop cadences and strong hooks of 'Hasta Mañana' – which was initially the first choice for the European Song Contest – have a real charm, thanks largely to the rich timbre and seemingly effortless vocal delivery of Agnetha.

One undoubted highlight is 'Dance While The Music Goes On', a stunning track, showcasing a Euro-disco sound that the band would come to embrace on their future albums.

Despite such gems, the second studio album is wildly diverse and erratic. This is the sound of a band still to fully realise their winning formula. But their star was in the ascendant.

Within a year, ABBA would nail their sound and secure their status as one of the most unique pop bands on the entire planet.

ABBA perform their hit 'Honey, Honey' in Germany, 28 September 1974

HITTING THE ROAD

Following Eurovision success with Waterloo, the first ABBA European tour met with mixed results

The year 1974 was absolutely pivotal for ABBA, but not just because of their famous performance and subsequent victory at the Eurovision Song Contest in Brighton; that same year would also witness the group's first European tour.

Preparations were already underway for their European sojourn, slated for November 1974, when ABBA made their first American television appearance on the *Mike Douglas Show*. Although the *Waterloo* album was just modestly successful at Number 145 on the Billboard 200, American critics were largely positive in their assessment of the work. *The Los Angeles Times*, for example, called it "...a compelling and fascinating debut album that captures the spirit of mainstream pop quite effectively...."

Riding the crest of the Eurovision wave, ABBA drew a collective breath, actually cancelling a 25-venue folk park tour that had been scheduled for the summer of 1974. Consideration was given for a lengthy tour that would include distant locales such as Israel, Yugoslavia, Turkey and Greece, but the idea was scrapped quickly because of perceptions that ABBA's hit base remained somewhat narrow.

The ABBA autumn 1974 tour kicked off on 17 November, with 21 dates booked in Denmark, Sweden, Germany, Austria, Norway and Finland. Rehearsals were conducted during two rigorous weeks from 5-15 November in Rudbecksskolan, Stockholm-Sollentuna. The first leg of the tour, with the initial concert in Copenhagen, followed by Hannover, Munich, Frankfurt, Berlin, Innsbruck, Vienna, and other cities, proved disappointing. Several shows failed to sell out, and a real reckoning occurred with the cancellation of an appearance in Zurich, Switzerland, due to an apparent lack of public interest.

Björn reflected on the sobering experience in *ABBA: The Book*, published in 2000. "We thought that we would be turning some people away here and there. Especially in Germany and in Austria, where our records were always at the top of the charts. We also thought that we would be singing in front of a younger audience. The majority of people in the crowd were at least 25 or 30 years old."

Left: The whole crew pictured together during the Sweden leg of the tour

ABBA – Thank You For The Music

Despite the turnout on the first leg of the tour, everyone acknowledged that a solid fan base remained in Denmark, West Germany and Austria, and the prospects for the second leg of the tour soon began to brighten when venues across Scandinavia started to sell out in January 1975.

Shows in eight cities, including Oslo, Stockholm, Lund, Vejle, Gothenburg, Helsinki, and a second appearance in Copenhagen, were enthusiastically received. Encouraged, ABBA swept into mid-year with 14 open-air dates booked across Sweden and Finland. More than 19,000 people attended a show at the amusement park Gröna Lund in Stockholm. Momentum was building fast.

Coinciding with the inaugural tour, the release of several singles in late 1974 slowly but surely helped ABBA's international star to rise. 'So Long' made the Top 10 in Austria and Sweden and Number 21 in Germany but failed

The band in London on the day they were set to embark on their European tour

Hitting the Road

A typically rainy day in London. The band were in the city for the premier of 'ABBA: The Movie'

The band hit the road in their tour bus with their driver, Hansi Schwarz

Posing for excited fans in Poland

to generate much buzz in the UK. The BBC's Radio 1 virtually ignored the release of 'I Do, I Do, I Do, I Do, I Do' in mid-1975. The catchy tune duly peaked at Number 38, yet it managed to capture Number 1 in South Africa and rose into the Top 5 across northern Europe.

Polar Music released the formidable foursome's third album, ABBA, on 21 April 1975, which included the future standards 'SOS' and 'Mamma Mia'. With that, the group's popularity in the UK surged as the 'Mamma Mia' single grabbed Number 1 and the 'SOS' single reached Number 6, while the album peaked at Number 13.

In Germany, 'Mamma Mia' made Number 1, and 'SOS' became ABBA's second top single. The success of 'SOS' continued, becoming ABBA's first Number 1 in France while making Number 2 in several other European countries as well.

In Canada, the ABBA power trio of hits peaked with 'SOS' at Number 9, 'I Do, I Do, I Do, I Do, I Do' at 12, and 'Mamma Mia' 18. In the crucial U.S. market, 'Mamma Mia' topped out at Number 32, while 'I Do, I Do, I Do, I Do, I Do' and 'SOS' both reached Number 15.

At the end of 1975, 'SOS' was recognised with a BMI (Broadcast Music, Inc.) Award as one of the most-played songs on radio stations across the United States. Still, the ABBA album did not generate tremendous excitement in the U.S., stalling at Number 174 on the Billboard 200 chart in spite of three hits in the market.

Perhaps nowhere was the reception of the ABBA album more enthusiastic than in Australia, which was destined to become an ABBA stronghold for years. The phenomenon of the music video, then in its embryonic stage across the world, fuelled an outpouring of interest as the televised popular music show *Countdown* aired the videos of 'I Do, I Do, I Do, I Do, I Do' and 'Mamma Mia'. With that, ABBA fever began to spread like wildfire. 'Mamma Mia' topped the charts in Australia for ten weeks, 'I Do, I Do, I Do, I Do, I Do' for three, and SOS for a week.

After a somewhat tentative and unsure first step with their European concert tour of 1974–1975, ABBA had finally found their footing.

Opposite top: A view of Gamleby Folkpark in Västervik, Sweden, during the ABBA Folkpark Tour 1975

Opposite: Boris Lindqvist joined the band's backing for 12 concerts in Germany, Austria and Switzerland

Hitting the Road

ABBA

On their genre-spanning third studio album, ABBA would define their signature sound and galvanise their reputation in the global marketplace

Things did not look too promising for ABBA in April 1975. Reviews were largely good, but recent UK singles had flopped and ticket sales for their live shows were slowing.

Salvation came in the form of their third, eponymous, studio album. This was the record on which ABBA found their true sound, their first really solid album and the one that would elevate them onto the international stage.

The album opens with 'Mamma Mia'. It's a barnstorming opener, a classic ABBA lyric of love gone wrong, set against double-tracked guitars and a strong marimba melody. 'Mamma Mia' is laden with hooks and impeccably arranged. At 0:50 the whole backing track drops out, leaving Agnetha and Frida singing the chorus line as the staccato piano pounds out the rhythm. At 1:04 there's a crack of snare before Rutger Gunnarsson's descending bass line underpins a new powerful refrain: "Yes I've been brokenhearted / blue since the day we started".

Lyrically, the album is upbeat, although as writer Jude Rogers noted in a BBC review in 2012, 'Mamma Mia' has dark lyrical undercurrents. "In it, we find one of ABBA's trademark sad, layered stories, bubbly and joyous to the ear, but full of darker details about "slammed doors", and an "angry and sad" woman that's "not that strong," she wrote.

By now, engineer and producer Michael B. Tretow had honed the band's sound. It's a testament to him that, almost five decades on, ABBA's songs still have such a sonic wallop and warmth.

Much of the dynamism of tracks such as 'Mamma Mia' comes from the piano lines. Tretow used three AKG C414 condenser mics to record the piano and was one of the first engineers to do this. The middle line was fed through an MXR flanger, then through a delay, resulting in an automatic pitch shift that became one of the band's signature techniques.

One of ABBA's key assets was the rhythm section of Rutger Gunnarsson (bass) and Ola Brunket (drums). Tretow would record Gunnarsson's bass in its own room, at peak volume, with a mic on the amp and an ambient mic placed outside the room. The same technique was used for Björn's guitar.

ABBA
RELEASED 21 April 1975
TRACKLIST

SIDE A
1. Mamma Mia
2. Hey, Hey Helen
3. Tropical Loveland
4. SOS
5. Man In The Middle
6. Bang-A-Boomerang

SIDE B
1. I Do, I Do, I Do, I Do, I Do
2. Rock Me
3. Intermezzo No. 1
4. I've Been Waiting For You
5. So Long

Tretow would place condenser mics on the drums to pick up the low sounds from Brunket's kit, which brought real heft to ABBA's sound.

This is the first album on which Björn and Benny barely sing, allowing the distinct vocal talents of Agnetha and Frida to come to the fore. Style-wise the album hurtles from genre to genre, but the shift in styles – from rock and reggae to prog, funk and classical – sounds sophisticated and assured.

This album yielded seven singles and surprisingly they released the weaker compositions first. Lyrically, the independent woman depicted in the narrative of 'So Long' is a welcome shift for ABBA, although its bouncy glam pop is a bizarre choice as the first single. The album's fourth single, 'Bang-A-Boomerang', is equally fizzy and upbeat, while the schmaltzy jazz-infused swing of 'I Do, I Do, I Do, I Do, I Do' has a strong, memorable hook.

Guitar riffage pervades 'Hey, Hey, Helen', a driving rock track about a woman who leaves her husband and children. Funky clavinet anchors the groove of 'Man In The Middle', while 'Intermezzo No. 1' showcases Björn and Benny's classical leanings.

But it wasn't until the album's sixth single, 'SOS', that the album started to yield some serious chart success. Released in June 1975, the track opens with a plaintive descending piano motif before a heartfelt vocal from Agnetha and a soaring chorus. Biographer Carl Magnus Palm described it as "Agnetha's first heartbreak classic, wherein the tear-filled vocal delivery, her trademark, would blend a pop melody with a dash of melancholy".

ABBA was the band's first strong album and the two singles 'Mamma Mia' and 'SOS' would become hits in Europe, the UK and the U.S. Björn would later say that 'SOS' was the moment when ABBA found their true identity. 'SOS' would rekindle their chart presence in the UK, where it reached Number 6, while the seventh single, 'Mamma Mia' would reach Number 1 in the UK, Germany and Australia. The album would yield three hit singles in the U.S. and prompt the American press to sit up and take notice. As *Creem* magazine put it, "'SOS' is surrounded on this LP by so many good tunes the mind boggles."

"I'M UNINTERESTED IN APPEARING IN NEWSPAPERS AND ON TV. IT'S JUST NOT SOMETHING I WANT TO DO. I OVERDOSED"

AGNETHA FÄLTSKOG
ON HER DESIRE TO AVOID THE SPOTLIGHT

ARRIVAL

Spawning three killer singles and oozing with confidence, ABBA's fourth album was an absolute classic

As cover concepts go, the image of the four rather pensive-looking members of Abba wedged into the cockpit of a Bell 47 helicopter isn't the most inspiring. But the shot, taken at the Barkarby Airport, northwest of Stockholm, does at least reflect the rarefied, globetrotting status that their burgeoning success was about to bestow upon them.

Arrival is the band's fourth studio long player and widely considered to be their first classic album. It contains three massive hit singles: 'Knowing Me, Knowing You', 'Money, Money, Money' and 'Dancing Queen'. Arrival marked the point at which everything moved up a gear for the band. Their growing confidence was echoed in their decision to use the now renowned mirror 'B' logo in the band's name. The sheer quality and consistency across the album would ensure that by 1977, as Pitchfork magazine put it, ABBA were "unshiftable, omnipresent and commercially invincible".

ABBA began working on the album in August 1975, and the first song they developed in the studio in Stockholm was 'Dancing Queen'. Initially entitled 'Boogaloo', it was inspired by the disco sound, particularly George McCrae's 'Rock Your Baby'. The backing track was laid down on 4 August, and from the outset the band knew they had something special. "We knew immediately it was going to be massive," recalled Agnetha. Anni-Frid was equally impressed. In an interview in 2021, she recalled Benny excitedly waking her when he returned from the studio, to play her the backing track.

"I started to cry," she recalled. "I was so moved by it because it was so beautiful, one of those songs that instantly goes straight into your heart… My favourite song has always been 'Dancing Queen'."

Almost five decades on from its release, 'Dancing Queen' remains one of the greatest pop songs ever recorded. From its dynamic sweeping piano intro and inspired melodic structure to the massive Spector-esque sound and the sublime vocal performances of Agnetha and Anni-Frid, 'Dancing Queen' is carefree, euphoric and triumphant yet tinged by what Björn has called "that Nordic melancholic feeling". Underpinning and weaving the whole composition together is a beautifully crafted bass line from session musician Rutger Gunnarsson, a masterclass in playing 'in the pocket' that helps to propel the song to incredible heights.

Arrival
RELEASED 11 October 1976
TRACKLIST

SIDE A
1. When I Kissed The Teacher
2. Dancing Queen
3. My Love, My Life
4. Dum Dum Diddle
5. Knowing Me, Knowing You

SIDE B
1. Money, Money, Money
2. That's Me
3. Why Did It Have To Be Me?
4. Tiger
5. Arrival

"Friday night and the lights are low," begins Agnetha, setting the scene for the song's character – a lonely, introspective 17 year old girl, on a nightclub dancefloor, lost in the music and the moment. Lyrically, it has emotional resonance for everyone, a song that reflects the travails and triumphs of life. "When we recorded the vocals, I remember we both had the chills," said Agnetha. "The hair stood up on our arms."

'Dancing Queen' would go on to be ABBA's biggest hit, reaching Number 1 in 15 countries, including the UK, the U.S., Sweden, the Soviet Union, Australia, Canada and South Africa.

Unlike previous albums, *Arrival* is strikingly consistent and assured. It also sounds like no one else. Opening track 'When I Kissed The Teacher' begins with rhythmic 12-string guitar before opening out into quirky, frenetic pop. 'Dum Dum Diddle' is equally idiosyncratic, a frivolous slice of bubblegum, which is redeemed by the vocals of Agnetha and Anni-Frid. By contrast, the title track is a potent, enigmatic soundscape with stirring Gaelic overtones, while the aching ballad 'My Love, My Life' is given real poignancy by Agnetha's vocals.

But inevitably, it's the singles that really shine on *Arrival*. 'Money. Money. Money' is another standout classic. Intro-ing with a staccato descending piano line, it's a clever arrangement with some nifty sonic gimmickry. It's lean, punchy and irrepressibly catchy and reached the Top 5 in numerous countries on its release as a single on 1 November 1976.

The third single, released on 18 February 1977, was 'Knowing Me, Knowing You', a bona fide ABBA classic, an uplifting slab of pop with an adult sensibility and the kind of joyous melancholy that had become a trademark of the ABBA sound. 'Breaking up is never easy I know / But I have to go' intones Frida.

Fuelled by three storming singles, *Arrival* stormed to Number 1 in nine countries on its release, including the UK, where it became the biggest-selling album of the year. It went on to peak at a respectable Number 20 on the U.S. Billboard Hot 100. With *Arrival*, ABBA had demonstrated their true commercial and creative worth. They were on the cusp of conquering the elusive U.S. market.

CHAPTER 3
MONEY, MONEY, MONEY

62 ABBA Mania

78 Discography: ABBA: The Album

80 Polar Music Studio

82 Across the Pond… and Back Again

89 Discography: Voulez-Vous

92 Discography: Super Trouper

Performing on America's hit late-night music TV show 'Midnight Special'

Inside the golden years of ABBA, when the fabulous foursome ruled the world...

What does superstardom really mean? In the case of ABBA, it meant a leap in profile from merely being successful musicians and singers – as Björn, Benny, Agnetha and Anni-Frid had been since the end of the 1960s – to being a brand, a logo, a list of names and group of faces that everyone knew.

And we do mean everyone. At ABBA's commercial peak, which we can reasonably identify as somewhere between 1979 and 1981, the group were a genuine cultural phenomenon. In pop music, a band as big as this comes along once a decade or so: see The Beatles in the 1960s, Duran Duran in the 1980s, the Spice Girls in the 1990s and perhaps One Direction in the 21st century.

Like most of those artists, ABBA's reign at the top of the music industry was relatively short, making this nostalgic look at their glory days not just entertaining or informative but also bittersweet.

While most bands end their careers with a singles compilation, ABBA did the opposite, kicking off their step-up to the stratosphere in 1976 with their first *Greatest Hits* album. A Number 1 hit in the UK and even penetrating the upper reaches of the stubborn American chart, the record was promoted with the single 'Fernando', which had previously been recorded by Anni-Frid for her 1975 solo album *Frida ensam* (Frida alone).

To say that 'Fernando' was greeted with worldwide

acclaim is selling it short. It's thought that this massively catchy – if unusual – song – a combination of Scandinavian wistfulness and red-hot Latin fervour – topped the charts in at least 13 countries and entered the Top 5 pretty much everywhere else. It's one of a small number of singles (less than 40) to sell over 10 million copies worldwide, which is more than many respectably sized bands achieve across their entire careers.

ABBA fever started in the UK and spread rapidly. Each country had its own brand of ABBA madness: in Australia, for example, 'Fernando' stayed at Number 1 for 14 weeks and stuck around on the chart for eight months. It was that continent's longest-running Number 1 until the arrival of Ed Sheeran 41 years later. In Germany, meanwhile, a local compilation called *The Very Best Of ABBA* hit Number 2 on the chart – only beaten by *Greatest Hits* itself.

Grabbing the opportunity to capitalise on this success, ABBA released their fourth album, *Arrival*, in October 1976. From the clever title, which implied that the band were a new sensation when in fact they had been around for some years, to the glamour implied by the helicopter in the artwork, the LP was designed to make an impact – and so it did.

As with *Greatest Hits* and 'Fernando', the numbers associated with *Arrival* are so huge that they become difficult to digest: it made Number 1 in the UK, Australia and several European countries, and Number 3 in Canada and Japan. Three singles were released from the album, which also included 'Fernando' in some territories: of these, 'Money, Money, Money' reached the top of the charts in Germany, France, Australia and elsewhere, while 'Knowing Me, Knowing You' scored Number 1 in the UK and Germany, ABBA's sixth consecutive single to do so in the latter country, a sign of their consistent popularity.

Arrival's biggest hit was a genuine behemoth – 'Dancing Queen', perhaps the epitome of this early, youthful bloom in ABBA's careers. It's easier to list the countries where the song was not a hit; let's just say that Number 1 scores in Canada, the Soviet Union, Mexico, South Africa and Japan were all signs that ABBA-mania was now truly global. Even the once stubborn U.S. couldn't resist, falling under ABBA's spell at this point too, the earworm melodies and lush textures of the music aligning with the wave of disco that was engulfing the American music-consuming public at the time.

Left: Promoting the incredible success of the 'Arrival' album

Right: Posing with a slightly unimpressed kangaroo in Australia

ABBA – Thank You For The Music

While ABBA weren't exactly a disco band as such, the funky bass and crisp drums that anchored the irrepressible vocal layers, and of course the shimmering, day-glo image of the band, certainly nodded in that direction.

The music industry – as always lagging behind the public by some way – was now starting to indicate a certain respect for ABBA, with rock-focused publications in the UK such as *Melody Maker* and *NME* giving the band positive reviews. The UK was on the cusp of being overwhelmed by the first wave of punk rock, a musical movement diametrically opposed in sound, image and ethos to that of ABBA: it's a mark of the Swedish group's charisma and skill that they retained a foothold even after that tidal wave broke.

By now, ABBA had also built a significant fanbase in Europe and Australasia, and a tour of those continents was scheduled for January 1977. At this point, the four Swedes had transcended their individual profiles and the group was recognised as a brand as much as a band, meaning that the forthcoming live dates had to be something very special indeed. On 28 January, the European and Australian Tour dates – titled rather unimaginatively by today's over-the-top standards – kicked off in Oslo, Norway, and attracted immediate interest for their extravagance.

As well as delivering the hits, ABBA included scenes from a theatrical opera performance, *The Girl With The Golden Hair*, which, again, might sound a touch naive from the

Rubbing shoulders with iconic British puppet Basil Brush, London, 1976

perspective of 2022 but which wowed crowds in Sweden, Denmark, Germany, Holland and finally in the ABBA-mad UK. There, the foursome played two sold-out concerts at London's Royal Albert Hall, one of which was filmed for posterity – a major undertaking in the analogue era. It's a sign of the Brits' love of ABBA that no fewer than three and a half million applications for tickets at the RAH were received, enough to sell it out 580 times. Why didn't ABBA play Wembley Arena, which had hosted up to 10,000 music fans at Beatles shows in the 1960s? Who knows...

While the European and British dates had been successful, the Australian leg of the tour was phenomenal. Why hundreds of thousands of sun-kissed Aussies should fall so deeply in love with the resolutely Scandinavian aura of ABBA has never been fully explained. Perhaps the relative lack of world-class Australian music in the late 1970s – AC/DC aside – meant that audiences Down Under hungered for sweeter, more sympathetic pop vibes than the guitar grind of their domestic bands? Whatever the cause, ABBA were

Left: Princess Margaret presents the group with the Carl-Alan Group Award for 1977 at the Lyceum Ballroom in London, England

huge in Australasia, and never bigger than at this particular point at the end of the decade of glam.

It's funny to think that ABBA travelled all the way to Australia, where fans were baying to hear them play, only to perform a mere 11 concerts. Nowadays, promoters and management would insist in maximising the tour's profitability with multiple nights at each venue. Still, ABBA gained exposure with that double handful of dates to over 160,000 people, gaining in profile along the way thanks to the quality of the shows and a few golden moments of comedy.

These included Anni-Frid slipping and falling to the stage during a rain-soaked concert at the Sydney Showground on 3 March: those high-heeled boots were evidently not designed for wet-weather grip, although it didn't prevent the four band members from labelling that 3 March gig as the most memorable of their collective careers.

The hysteria grew as the tour progressed to Melbourne, where ABBA were afforded a civic reception and waved regally from the balcony of the Town Hall to a gathering

Waving to screaming Australian fans at Melbourne Airport, 1977

of 6,000 fans. Three shows were performed at the Sidney Myer Music Bowl, with the Australian Prime Minister Malcolm Fraser and his family among the 14,500-strong faithful who were lucky enough to get in: at the first of those concerts, no fewer than 16,000 fans hung around outside the venue to listen. The pattern was repeated in Adelaide, where 20,000 fans got in – and 10,000 more did not.

The Aussie dates were attended by controversy when a bomb scare in Perth meant that the Entertainment Centre venue had to be evacuated. A less threatening and more frivolous moment came when Agnetha was obliged to defend her skimpy stage costume with the words "Don't they have bottoms in Australia?" Much of this drama was captured in *ABBA: The Movie*, directed by the acclaimed film-maker Lasse Hallström, a documentary that remains absolutely essential viewing for anyone interested in the huge cultural impact of ABBA in this far-off time and place.

To tie in with *ABBA: The Movie*, the group released their fifth LP, *ABBA: The Album*, at the end of 1977. While it was unrealistic to expect that the album could elevate the group to even higher levels of exposure, because they had already become celebrities on a global level, it did contain two worldwide hits in the singles 'The Name Of The Game' and 'Take A Chance On Me'. Both songs are more thoughtful and less extrovert in nature than earlier hits such as 'Dancing Queen', for example, which celebrated the simple pleasures of nightlife; the new songs were respectively more reflective and more vulnerable in theme.

'The Name Of The Game' entered the Top 5 in much of Europe and Australasia and hovered in the upper charts in North America; 'Take A Chance On Me' was even bigger, topping charts or coming close to doing so in Europe, the U.S. and Canada and making the Top 10 in disparate territories. The latter release became ABBA's biggest American hit, although it marked the beginning of the end of Australia's passionate love affair with the band, making a modest impact there rather than a seismic one. A third single, 'Eagle', was a lesser but still notable hit in many countries, although its B-side (remember them?) was 'Thank You For The Music', a massive hit when it was released six years later to an ABBA-free world.

Of course, that situation was virtually unthinkable back in 1977 and '78, given the stories that circulated at the time of *ABBA: The Album* exceeding a million copies in the Iron Curtain state of Poland and Soviet Russian pressing plants being unable to meet the demand of the public for the record. How could ABBA ever fall from grace, given their commercial status? Few bands had ever gripped the public attention with greater fervour, and interest in the musicians' personal lives was intense: the marriage of Benny and Anni-Frid on 6 October 1978 was headline news, for example.

Right: **The band stand in front of a billboard of themselves in Los Angeles, U.S., 1978**

Anni-Frid with excited young fans in Stockholm, 1978

To reinforce this total dominance, in the spring of 1979 the quartet announced a new album, *Voulez-Vous*, to be followed by ABBA: The Tour, a live run through North America, Europe and Asia that would extend from September that year into March 1980. The new album had its fair share of songs that have gone on to be classics, three of which were released as singles – 'Chiquitita', 'Does Your Mother Know?' and the anthemic 'I Have A Dream' – alongside the lesser-known but still worthy 'Angeleyes', 'Good As New' and the album's title track.

As you can read elsewhere in this publication, the background to *Voulez-Vous* was chaotic to say the least, but this didn't seem to affect the production of the tour – ABBA's last, as it turned out – or its reception by the public. Once again this six-month, 52-date outing didn't exactly have the most compelling title, with varying territories giving it functional titles such as 'ABBA in Concert' and 'ABBA: North American & European Tour 1979', but again, nothing could slow down these victorious musicians on their final lap.

Preparations for the tour took up the summer of 1979, with Agnetha and Anni-Frid taking vocal lessons, full-production rehearsals and a huge media blitz: *Billboard* magazine even ran a 50-page mini-magazine about ABBA in its 8 September issue.

ABBA: The Tour began its run in Edmonton in the Canadian province of Alberta on 13 September and rapidly rolled through Vancouver, Seattle, Portland, Concord, Anaheim and San Diego before heading into the American interior, with shows in Tempe, Las Vegas, Omaha, Saint Paul, Milwaukee and Chicago. The continental east coast – New York City, Boston, Montreal and Toronto – wound up the North American leg, but the final show was cancelled after a terrifying flight from New York to Boston during which ABBA's private plane endured rough weather, leaving Agnetha's nerves in tatters.

Benny was aware of the strains caused by these giant tours, saying some years later, "If you look at *ABBA: The Movie*, you'll see that Agnetha was never quite able to let go on stage. She was always a bit fearful – whereas Frida is clearly having a whale of a time."

In her 1997 autobiography, *As I Am*, Agnetha confirmed this, saying, "Sometimes it was awful. I felt as if [the fans] would get hold of me and I'd never get away again. It was as if I was going to be crushed. No one who has experienced facing a screaming, boiling, hysterical crowd could avoid feeling shivers up and down their spine. It's a thin line between ecstatic celebration and menace."

Shortly into the tour, Björn and Benny revealed some nerves of their own, saying "To us, the U.S. is mainly a challenge. The whole tour to us is a great challenge. Tonight, the audience was great and everything went smoothly. But it was a very strange feeling when we have not toured in two and a half years. You don't have the self-confidence that most artists have that tour a lot, and you don't know until you're up there, until you meet the audience face to face, whether it's going to work or not."

They had no need to worry, though, as the response was largely positive, critically and commercially. On 19 October, ABBA began their European dates in Gothenburg and Stockholm, following up with shows in Denmark, France, Holland, Germany, Switzerland, Austria and Belgium. This time, when they visited the UK, they made a point of selling out London's Wembley Arena: no medium-sized Royal Albert Hall shows were planned this time, although a stop-off at Stafford before dates in Glasgow and Dublin was a little unusual given the band's huge status. ABBA then flew to Japan to finish their enormous tour, commencing with one of three Tokyo gigs on 12 March 1980 and playing Fukuoka, Osaka and Nagoya.

The four musicians must have been exhausted, as the show required maximum engagement from them. Throughout the 40-city run, the set list had kicked off each night with an instrumental, 'Gammal Fäbodpsalm', before around 25 songs made up of new material from *Voulez-Vous* and established favourites. They would have relished

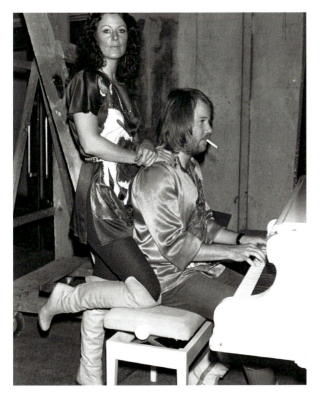

Frida and Benny backstage at a television show in Paris, 1978

Recording a music video in Switzerland, 1979

the mid-set break permitted them when backing singer Tomas Ledin stepped up to sing 'Not Bad At All', as well as the instrumental interlude 'Intermezzo No. 1', of course, but the logistical effort required for 'I Have A Dream' – performed with a local children's choir from the city in which they were playing – must have been considerable. Agnetha's solo rendition at the piano of 'I'm Still Alive' must have been draining for her, too.

There was comedy, though. Asked if he remembered any embarrassing moments on stage, Björn recalled, "The most embarrassing moment was on stage in Melbourne. I was talking to Benny on stage, [bantering] back and forth and this word came, I don't know from where, but I called him a bastard. I meant to say 'You silly man' or something and I said 'bastard' and I could hear [a shocked intake of breath] from 15,000 people. That was my worst moment on stage."

By the time the group made it to the encores of 'Dancing Queen' and 'Waterloo', the sense of relief would have been palpable. Fans who demanded more from the band than a single show could usually go and see *ABBA: The Movie*, which was screened locally after each gig in a cunning business move by the band and their management.

Talking of movies, the massive tour was celebrated in fine – and lasting – style with *ABBA In Concert*, a film of the Wembley Arena show: this was screened on UK and U.S. television the following year before a release on videocassette. You can now get it on DVD or as part of a 2014 box set called *Live At Wembley Arena*, meaning that ABBA's legendary run across the globe at the peak of their powers is committed to the record permanently, fortunately for the group's millions of modern-day followers.

That was it for ABBA as a live act, it seemed. Looking back, Björn told interviewer Jim Irvin, "We only had two major tours. I don't think we toured more than six months in total. I didn't like touring. We felt it was bad for creativity, reproducing the songs, screaming fans, dinner, parties, the same thing every night, every country, and then after that you wake up and travel to the next city, when the most important thing you could be doing was writing new songs. [That] is why we turned down lots of offers to tour. We did the right thing, I'm sure, because so many bands dry up when they're touring too much."

It's reasonable to state that ABBA's immense profile plateaued at this point, but that's hardly an indication of failure: how any musical group could get any bigger than this is genuinely hard to fathom. When 'The Winner Takes It All' was released as a single in July 1980, it fuelled rumours that it was about divorce within the band – which

Above: Björn and Agnetha skating at Leysin Sports Centre ice rink during the filming of their first television special, 'ABBA In Switzerland'

it was not – and appealed to the band's maturing fanbase, many of whom had now been following ABBA for three or four years.

Asked about 'The Winner Takes It All', Björn explained, "I sang a demo of it myself, which a lot of people liked and said, 'You have to sing that'. But I saw the sensible thing of course; it had to go to Agnetha. I remember coming to the studio with it and everyone said, 'Oh this is great, wonderful'. It was strange hearing her singing it. It was more like an actress doing something when she sang it, but deeply moving... Afterwards there were a few tears as well. I remember I wrote that lyric very quickly, which was rare with me. I was drunk – I'd been drinking Scotch – and it came in one hour. And that never works, writing when you're drunk; you think it's wonderful but it looks terrible the next day – but that one worked."

Left: Performing at The Music for UNICEF Concert: A Gift of Song benefit concert, held at the United Nations General Assembly in New York City, 9 January 1979

The song made the Top 10 in the U.S. and became ABBA's second Billboard Adult Contemporary chart-topper – 'Adult' being the operative word now that the musicians were in more sophisticated mode. This evolution was reflected still further in ABBA's seventh album, *Super Trouper*, released in November 1980 and – despite its none-too-serious title – the group's most reflective to date. This applied to the arrangements, such as the clever vocal intro of the title cut, and to the wall-of-sound layers of music, as in the single 'Lay All Your Love On Me'. With a million preorders in the UK, the LP was destined to be a huge hit.

Although in hindsight we can see that ABBA's first period of golden stardom was on the wane as 1980 became 1981, the minds behind the organisation were as busy as ever. In a genius business move that has been often emulated since then, the group recorded an LP of Spanish-language versions of their hits for release in Latin America. The album, *Gracias Por La Música*, was the logical conclusion of ABBA's earlier flirtations with Latino themes in 'Fernando' and 'Chiquitita' and opened up a whole new continent of fans for them.

In April 1981 ABBA released album number eight, *The Visitors*, with a title track that indirectly criticised Soviet totalitarianism, while other songs addressed mature themes such as the onset of age and the failure of relationships. This was a long way from the ABBA of the 'Ring Ring' days, and while there are pop melodies aplenty on the record, it's not clear that ABBA's fans wanted their band to step up to this level of considered songwriting. Still, the beautiful 'One Of Us' and an aptly titled last American hit, 'When All Is Said And Done', revealed that ABBA's collective songwriting and performance abilities remained undimmed.

1982 started well, with three new songs – 'You Owe Me One', 'I Am The City' and 'Just Like That' – written and recorded in the early summer, but Benny and Björn felt that they lacked a certain something and the tapes were shelved. Plans for a new studio album were also set aside: instead, it was agreed that a double-LP compilation should be assembled in time for Christmas. The result, *The Singles: The First Ten Years*, was accompanied by the singles 'The Day Before You Came' and 'Under Attack', but it's telling that neither broke into the Top 20 in ABBA's commercial heartland, the UK. Perhaps the times had changed: in 1982, pop fans now had new and exciting music to listen to from Duran Duran and Adam & The Ants, whose look and sound was more modern and just as catchy as anything by ABBA.

The Swedes didn't take this personally, though, and came to London to promote *The Singles: The First Ten Years* in November '82, performing on Saturday Superstore before heading to Germany to appear on *Show Express*. On 19 November they appeared for the last time in Sweden on a TV programme called *Nöjesmaskinen*, and on 11 December their last-ever performance was broadcast to the UK on Noel Edmonds' *The Late, Late Breakfast Show* via a live link from a studio in Stockholm.

Of course, by 'last-ever performance' we only mean the final, all-singing-all-dancing musical show. The foursome have appeared together many times since then, but not necessarily on a public broadcast or actually playing music – and as we'll see, they have been present in one form or other more or less constantly since their first decade of fame.

One last note. When we try to understand ABBA's enormous cultural impact in the late 1970s so many years after the fact, we have to acknowledge that a presence as huge as theirs never really goes away.

Of course, ABBA's popularity has waxed and waned over the decades: as we'll see, the 1980s weren't kind to their music, but from the mid-1990s onward, public appetite for the band and their music has slowly and steadily increased. Reunions or no reunions, ABBA are here to stay.

Right: **The group in Paris, France, in 1979**

Dockside in the Gamla Stan (Old Town) of Stockholm, Sweden, July 1977

ABBA: THE ALBUM

ABBA's fifth studio album marked a real step forward for the band as they embraced rock music like never before

By their fifth studio album, Björn, Benny, Agnetha and Anni-Frid had moved away from their Europop sound and embraced rock, notably the laidback Californian strains of Fleetwood Mac and various prog ensembles. But their pop sensibilities remained intact as evidenced by the huge popularity of this album and the two massive singles it yielded – 'Take A Chance On Me' and 'The Name Of The Game'.

Synthesisers are at the fore on the album's opener 'Eagle', an assured, pulsating track that melds big production with prog and ambient flourishes. Lyrically, all references to dancefloor euphoria are gone, replaced instead by heavier themes such as power and freedom.

ABBA: The Album
RELEASED 12 December 1977
TRACKLIST

SIDE A
1. Eagle
2. Take A Chance On Me
3. One Man, One Woman
4. The Name Of The Game

SIDE B
1. Move On
2. Hole In Your Soul
3. Thank You For The Music
4. I Wonder (Departure)
5. I'm A Marionette

A rhythmic a cappella intros the next track, 'Take A Chance On Me', which was the second single, released in January 1978. It's an infectious, richly layered song, with enthralling vocal harmonies from Agnetha and Anni-Frid. Once again, Björn and Benny demonstrate their unique prowess as songwriters, arrangers and producers, meticulously adding sounds and motifs that enhance yet never clutter, striving for melodic heights and always serving the song.

There are distinct 'lighters-in-the-air' moments on 'One Woman, One Man', an unashamed power ballad, with rapid-fire piano chords from Benny and slick synths and soaring electric guitar dominating the instrumental sections.

An infectious groove anchors 'The Name Of The Game', which was released as the album's first single on 17 October 1977. It's a track that sounds so generically AOR at times that only the distinctive vocals of Agnetha and Anni-Frid remind the listener that this is, in fact, ABBA. Despite the big production, it's warm and spacious, with powerful harmonies and inspired brass refrains.

The strong rock influence on the album is evident on 'Hole In Your Soul', a 4/4 foot-to-the-floor stomper with crunching riffs, searing lead guitar and some daft but endearing lyrics: "It's got to be rock 'n' roll / That fills the hole in your soul" sing Agnetha and Frida on the chorus.

'Move On', by comparison, is a quirky, curious hybrid, opening with echo-drenched electric piano and smatterings of vibrato flute. On the first verse, Björn speaks the lyrics, which makes it sound like some kitsch country music confessional melded with a space-age spiritual.

"They say a restless body can hide a peaceful soul," he begins, sounding like an intergalactic George Jones. "A

Discography: ABBA The Album

voyager, and a settler, they both have a distant goal."

When Agnetha and Anni-Frid enter the mix, however, the song assumes a far more plaintive and poignant feel.

The final three songs on the album – 'Thank You For The Music', 'I Wonder (Departure)' and 'I Am A Marionette', were part of *The Girl With The Golden Hair: Three Scenes From A Mini Musical*. This was an example of Björn and Benny flexing their creative wings. While their suite of songs certainly has its merits, its inclusion on the album feels disjointed, and critics and fans were less than impressed.

ABBA: The Album was released on 12 December 1977 in Sweden in conjunction with *ABBA: The Movie*. Its release was delayed until January 1978 in the UK due to pressing plants being unable to meet the colossal pre-order demand. The album reached Number 1 in numerous territories, including the UK, where it debuted at the top of the charts and stayed there for seven weeks. In the U.S., it reached Number 14, the highest position in the U.S. for any ABBA album at the time. The singles 'The Name Of The Game' and 'Take A Chance On Me' both reached Number 1 in the UK, with the latter peaking in the Top 5 in the U.S.

Critics hailed the album. John Rockwell from *Rolling Stone* applauded the band's stylistic shift from "innocently superficial lyrics, bouncy Europop music, rock energy and amplification, soaring melodies" to a more mature and intelligent record. It was a view shared by Bruce Eder from *AllMusic*, who gave the album four out of five stars, acknowledging that ABBA's profound shift in style was a result of "absorbing and assimilating some of the influences around them… without compromising their essential virtues as a pop ensemble".

ABBA – Thank You For The Music

POLAR MUSIC
STUDIO

A peek inside the magicians' grotto – the legendary Polar Studios in Stockholm

Polar Music Studio

Every scientist needs a laboratory, and while the great brains behind ABBA are best described as creative rather than scientific, the analogy holds up, because the musical alchemy that took place in the fabled Polar Studios, now extant in name and reputation only, was synonymous with the location where it took place.

If you happened to be walking down the Stockholm street of Kungsholmen at any time between 18 May 1978 and as recently as 2004, you might find yourself hearing the sound of music emanating from a massive building at Sankt Eriksgatan 58-60 called the Sportpalatset, which translates as Palace Of Sports. Of course, only the music made there from 1978 to approximately 1982 was truly ABBA-esque in nature; after that, you would still have heard albums being recorded inside the 1930s-built edifice, but they would have sounded rather different.

The decision to build a studio in the Sportpalatset back in '77 came about when Björn, Benny, Agnetha and Anni-Frid – plus their ever-canny manager Stig Anderson, owner of the Polar Music label – realised that a studio devoted solely to ABBA would be both convenient and cost-effective. To achieve the huge layers of vocals that the band required a large recording space was needed, hence the choice of building, which had previously functioned as a cinema.

To this end, a large chunk of ABBA's earnings were invested in state-of-the-art recording equipment. Two rooms, Studio A and Studio B, were fitted out with a Harrison mixing console, which – for those of us who have no idea what that means – functions very like the industry standard, a near-priceless Neve desk.

Apparently aware years before everyone else that digital recording was the future but that old-school analogue recording still had some years left to it, ABBA opted to equip the studios with both options: in 1981, they recorded their album *The Visitors*, the third of three LPs cut there, on

Left: Björn and Benny record a track in the studio. The walls are adorned with the band's many gold and platinum records

Technician Michael Tretow in the studio with musicians Rutger Gunnarsson, Ola Brunkert, Lasse Wellander and Benny and Björn

a 3M digital recorder, becoming one of the first pop bands to do so. If you've ever wondered why ABBA's later songs sound so flawless, now you know the answer.

ABBA made Polar Studios their home for several years, recording solo albums there long after the dissolution of the parent band – and Anderson wasn't slow to invite other groups to record there. Impressed with the crystal-clear Polar sound and the vast dimensions of the facility, Led Zeppelin recorded *In Through The Out Door* (their eighth and ultimately final studio album) there in 1979, and Genesis followed a year later with their *Duke* LP.

Artists such as Roxy Music, Adam Ant, the Beastie Boys, Celine Dion, Roxette and Joan Armatrading followed suit, even though by the mid-1980s the studio had been sold to Anderson's daughter Marie Ledin and the ABBA connection had been effectively severed.

Rising rent costs forced the studio out in 2004, and the business was scaled down a few years later, but the Polar experience lived on in a 2010 exhibition at ABBA The Museum – and you can always watch the video for 'Gimme! Gimme! Gimme! (A Man After Midnight)', which was shot there in the studio's heyday. It's a trip back in time…

ABBA – Thank You For The Music

ACROSS THE POND AND BACK AGAIN

The 1979 North American and European Tour brought varied results

Across The Pond And Back Again

By the late 1970s, ABBA were without doubt one of the most popular music groups in the world. Nevertheless, studio quality and live performance road warrior triumph were poles apart for the famed foursome.

Success had been steady with the debut of their *Greatest Hits* album in the spring of 1976, which maintained ABBA's position of prominence in Europe and Australia while the group reached the Top 50 on the album charts in the United States for the first time. The single 'Fernando' rose to Number 13 on the Billboard Top 100 in the U.S. Still, the heights of stardom in the United States remained elusive, even after the release of the group's fourth album, *Arrival*, in October 1976. Three hits brought acclaim for *Arrival*, including 'Dancing Queen', 'Knowing Me, Knowing You', and 'Money, Money, Money'. While these topped the charts in Europe, only 'Dancing Queen' reached Number 1 on the Billboard Hot 100 in the U.S., while 'Knowing Me, Knowing You' climbed to Number 7, and 'Money, Money, Money' failed to gain traction at all.

Interestingly, though, *Arrival*'s three biggest hits each made Number 1 in more focused U.S. charts, such as Adult Contemporary and Hot Club Dance Play. Therefore, *Arrival* proved to be a major stepping stone toward broader popularity in the United States and Canada. As a result the album must be considered a breakthrough with its peak at Number 20 on the Billboard 200 chart. The album was certified gold by the Recording Industry Association of America.

The release of *ABBA: The Album*, the group's fifth, and *ABBA: The Movie* accompanied the group's 1977 European and Australian Tour. Worldwide airplay continued with 'Take A Chance On Me' and 'The Name Of The

On stage at the Auditorium Theater in Chicago, Illinois, U.S., 30 September 1979

Game'. By early 1979, ABBA had performed alongside Donna Summer, Earth, Wind & Fire, Olivia Newton-John and the Bee Gees in New York City during a charity event for UNICEF. In April, the group's sixth album, *Voulez-Vous*, was released, cracking the Top 20 in the U.S. and the Top 10 in Canada with singles 'Chiquitita' and 'Does Your Mother Know'.

Still, something else was glittering in the proverbial distance. The question lingered... could ABBA achieve superstardom in North America on the same scale as they had in Europe? Plans for a lengthy world tour originally included Western and Eastern Europe, Asia and North America, but these were later reduced to allow more time to finish *Voulez-Vous* in the studio. As it developed, the North American and European Tour of 1979 would last seven months and stretch into the following year, while the only Asian dates remaining were set for Japan.

Rehearsals for the 1979 tour began in mid-May at the Stockholm Concert Hall, and an elaborate stage design including 40-50 tons of equipment was assembled. The setup would require three large trucks for overland transportation. Two surprise concerts took place at Stockholm venues to help build confidence since, frankly, the group had mixed emotions regarding live performances and did not tour as extensively as other superstar bands.

In the 2000 book *From ABBA to Mamma Mia!*, Benny was quoted on the two surprise shows: "We tour so infrequently that we need to have a little warm up. Especially since we're going to the United States where we've never been before and where we're all a bit unsure of how the audience regards us: whether they are familiar with us or not. We really don't know, so we need a little extra self-confidence as a stage act."

The pre-tour hype got into full swing as *Billboard* magazine published a 50-page promotional insert in its 8 September

Meeting and greeting fans in Paris, France

Agnetha performs on stage at Ahoy in Rotterdam, Netherlands, October 1979

1979 issue, which included interviews with Benny and other band members Björn, Agnetha and Anni-Frid. Along the way, Benny and Björn were candid, commenting, "To us, the U.S. is mainly a challenge. The whole tour to us is a great challenge. Tonight, the audience was great and everything went smoothly. But it was a very strange feeling when we have not toured in two and a half years. You don't have the self-confidence that most artists have that tour a lot and you don't know until you're up there, until you meet the audience face-to-face, whether it's going to work or not...."

The widely anticipated tour opened to a packed house of 14,000 at the Northlands Coliseum in Edmonton, Alberta, Canada, on 13 September 1979. Edmonton was the first of 45 appearances in North America and Europe that year, and, blazing the trail across Canada and the U.S., ABBA played 17 dates to houses that sold out. Thirteen of these were in the U.S. and four in Canada, buoying hopes that the group would indeed find the mega-stardom in North America that had long been evident across Western Europe. Other cities included Vancouver, Seattle, Portland, Anaheim, San Diego, Las Vegas, Omaha, St. Paul, Chicago, New York, Montreal and Toronto.

Nevertheless, there were some disappointments along the way. The group was literally shaken during violent weather while flying in their private jet from New York to Boston, arriving for their show at the Boston Music Hall on 3 October 1979, an hour and a half late. The flight had been so unnerving, particularly for Agnetha, that a follow-on Washington, D.C., concert was cancelled.

The 45 shows during the year drew 300,000 fans, but still some of the concerts in the U.S. did not sell out completely. Here and there the reviews ran the spectrum from sublime to derogatory. And perhaps most significant of all, the net revenue resulted in a loss of about $200,000.

The Edmonton Journal had gushed following the opening concert, "The voices of the band, Agnetha's high sauciness combined with the round, rich lower tones of

Anni-Frid and Benny get the crowd going in Rotterdam

Anni-Frid, were excellent... Technically perfect, melodically correct and always in perfect pitch... The soft lower voice of Anni-Frid and the high, edgy vocals of Agnetha were stunning."

But another critic who attended the same Edmonton show had, perhaps, sensed some of the personal drama and the ongoing struggle for onstage confidence, writing, "...During the first half, the performers lacked the supercharged vitality and provocative self-assurance normally associated with big-league artists. However, for cool professionalism, assembly line precision and computer-perfect programming, the show functioned like a machine from start to finish."

Indeed, Björn and Agnetha had announced their divorce in January 1979. Its sombre shadow no doubt influenced the preparations and the performances during the tour. The first of the ABBA four to tell her own story, Agnetha wrote in her 1997 book *As I Am ABBA: Before and Beyond*, "I hadn't reached this level of maturity when we began the USA tour of 1979... It was momentous and successful, but for me it was awful. Björn and I had separated and I had torn myself away from the children [Linda and Peter].

"I just wanted to be home, home, home. But I had no choice... It was an unfamiliar situation for all of us – an ordeal by fire... The whole time I ached inside for the children and from home sickness."

After the North American dates, ABBA played to their Western European power base with shows in 23 cities, including Gothenburg, Stockholm, Copenhagen, Paris, Rotterdam, Dortmund, Munich, Zurich, Vienna, Brussels, London, Glasgow and Dublin. In March 1980, ABBA toured Japan, with appearances in Tokyo, Fukuoka, Kōriyama, Osaka and Nagoya.

Surely, there was some solace in the return to familiar territory. Twenty-three shows of the European tour leg were sellouts, including six performances at London's Wembley Stadium. Further, the greeting ABBA received at the airport in Tokyo as thousands of screaming fans crowded close must have been heartening. All 11 concerts in Japan, including six at the famed Nippon Budokan Theater, sold out.

The tour had proved yet again just how immensely popular ABBA remained across the globe, their catchy songs and vibrant performances transcending cultural and language barriers everywhere. And yet, despite their status as a pop phenomenon being cemented beyond doubt, the tour of 1979 would prove to be their last.

ABBA perform with the Bee Gees and Rita Coolidge for a 1979 UNICEF song

Across The Pond And Back Again

VOULEZ-VOUS

The resurgence of disco was fully embraced by the band on their sixth album, a release that presented their biggest challenges to date

By 1978, ABBA had become a phenomenon, with sell-out tours, Number 1 hits, a blockbuster movie and an adoring global fanbase. For Björn and Benny, however, the sixth album was the catalyst for a creative block. Tensions weren't helped by Björn and Agnetha's disintegrating relationship, which would result in the break-up of their marriage in 1980.

It's fair to say that *Voulez-Vous* would sound nothing like it does were it not for the Bee Gees. In 1977 disco experienced a renaissance thanks to the colossal popularity of the Bee Gees' *Saturday Night Fever*, and its influence can be felt across *Voulez-Vous*.

Lyrically, the pain of Björn and Agnetha's break-up permeated the album. Gone were third-person narratives of dancefloor disaffection. In their place were more barbed first-person accounts of splitting up and moving out. Opening track 'As Good As New' set the tone: "I'll never know why I had to go," begins Agnetha. "Why I had to put up such a lousy rotten show / Boy, I was tough, packing all my stuff / Saying I don't need you anymore, I've had enough".

The song intros with staccato strings before lurching at 0:15 into a jagged, frenetic funk groove, complete with slap bass. When Agnetha's voice enters the mix at 0:29 it sounds rich and dynamic.

Title track 'Voulez-Vous' continues the lyrical theme, detailing the scenario of lonely souls looking for love in clubs and bars. "I know what you think / The girl means business, so I'll offer her a drink / Lookin' mighty proud / See you leave your table, pushing through the crowd."

Most of the instrumental backing for the title track was recorded at Criteria Studios in Miami, where the Bee Gees' mega-hit had been recorded. At the end of January 1978, Björn and Benny rented an apartment in the Bahamas to allow them to focus on soaking up American music away from the conservative confines of Stockholm.

The experiment worked. 'Voulez-Vous', the only ABBA track to be recorded outside Sweden, is a fast and furious slice of Chic-styled disco, with powerful guitars and dexterous disco bass from Arnold Paseiro of Latin/

Voulez-Vous
RELEASED 23 March 1978
TRACKLIST

SIDE A
1. As Good As New
2. Voulez-Vous
3. Have A Dream
4. Angeleyes
5. The King Has Lost His Crown

SIDE B
1. Does Your Mother Know
2. If It Wasn't For The Nights
3. Chiquitita
4. Lovers (Live A Little Longer)
5. Kisses Of Fire

disco band Foxy. Production is sleek and there's an enigmatic feel to the vocals of Agnetha and Anni-Frid. "What I had in mind before I even had the title was a kind of nightclub scene, with a certain amount of sexual tension and eyes looking at each other," said Björn. Released as a single in 1979, it reached the Top 5 on charts across Europe, peaking at Number 3 in the ABBA-mad UK.

The gutsy, storming 'Summer Night City' continues the stomping upbeat disco vibe, while 'The King Has Lost His Crown' continues the rather embittered lyrical tone. The pristine Europop of 'Angeleyes' is also aimed squarely at a former lover.

In addition to disco-fuelled tracks, the album contains some soft, lyrical Europop ballads, a reminder of Agnetha and Anni-Frid's folk music roots in the mid- to late-'60s.

The Latin-tinged ballad 'Chiquitita', with its flowing piano and Spanish guitar flourishes, highlights the purity of Agnetha's voice. It's a beautiful track, which begins with a slow, sparse feel before the 'oompah' rhythm of the European folk tradition enters the mix. Released as the first single from the album, it reached Number 1 in the UK, Holland, Belgium and Switzerland.

'I Have A Dream', the sixth and final single, is utopian-themed, featuring the lush vocal vibrato of Frida against a blissfully simple arrangement, including 12-string acoustic guitar.

By complete contrast, a crunching rock-guitar riff intros 'Does Your Mother Know?', a pulsating 4/4 dance-rock track that reached Number 4 in the UK when it was released as the second single.

'Voulez-Vous' was released on 23 April 1979 and topped the charts in the UK and across Europe. Benny and Björn had overcome their creative block and produced a majestic, shimmering work yielding six impressive singles. Over four decades on, it remains a high point in the band's illustrious back catalogue.

"THE MUSIC OF ABBA IS NOT THAT HAPPY. IT MIGHT SOUND HAPPY, BUT DEEP WITHIN IT'S NOT. WHAT FOOLS YOU IS THE GIRLS' VOICES"

BJÖRN ULVAEUS
ON THE HIDDEN SORROW WITHIN ABBA'S WORK

SUPER TROUPER

The raw emotion of imploding relationships inspires this powerful and intense collection of songs

The dawning of a new decade brought with it a shift in style for ABBA, who wisely eschewed the dwindling disco and returned instead to the pop-rock sound of their earlier albums. There's a darkness to this release, informed by the break-up of Björn and Agnetha's marriage. As they began work on Super Trouper in February 1980, Benny and Frida's relationship was also imploding. By the time the first copies of the album hit the stores on 3 November, their separation had been finalised.

Not surprisingly, a spirit of introspection pervades. ABBA always managed to transform melancholy into sonic gold dust and here they take it up a notch. The result is a strong album, steeped in emotion and honesty, and boasting some sublime moments across its ten tightly produced tracks.

Ballads dominate the release, as evidenced by the contemplative 'Happy New Year', one of the songs written in January 1980 when Björn and Benny revisited Barbados to write. The verse is reminiscent of a song from a stage musical but the chorus is trademark ABBA, and the upbeat melodicism is offset by quiet Nordic melancholy. "May we all have our hopes / Our will to try / If we don't we might as well lay down and die".

'Andante, Andante', the first track to be recorded, is a lush waltzy ballad, with flowery piano arpeggios. Sung by Frida, it focuses on the consummation of a love affair, recounted metaphorically via musical instructions. Both songs were among the seven tracks released as singles from the album. The biggest single of all was another ballad, 'The Winner Takes It All'.

Released as a lead single months in advance of the album, 'The Winner Takes It All' was a global smash, a heart-wrenching ballad that reached the Top 10 in every major market in the world. The track is regularly voted the best ABBA single in polls, a view shared by Agnetha, who also delivers an astonishing vocal performance.

Benny and Björn started writing the song in the summer of 1979 in a cottage on the island of Viggsö. "I was drunk, and the whole lyric came to me in a rush of emotion in one hour," recalled Björn. When he showed the lyrics to Agnetha he recalled that "a tear or two welled up in her eyes. Because the words really affected her".

The song is frequently voted the best break-up song ever. "I was in your arms / Thinking I belonged there / I figured it

Super Trouper
RELEASED 3 November 1980
TRACKLIST

SIDE A
1. Super Trouper
2. The Winner Takes It All
3. On And On And On
4. Andante, Andante
5. Me and I

SIDE B
1. Happy New Year
2. Our Last Summer
3. The Piper
4. Lay All Your Love On Me
5. The Way Old Friends Do (live)

made sense / Building me a fence / Building me a home / Thinking I'd be strong there / But I was a fool / Playing by the rules."

A teenage romance in Paris was Björn's lyrical inspiration for 'Our Last Summer', a plaintive ballad sung by Frida. The song was not released as a single but its status was boosted by its use in the 2008 film *Mamma Mia!*.

Another real highlight is the title track 'Super Trouper', a soaring, strident pop-rock song that opens the album. The track begins with the echo-drenched a cappella harmonies of Agnetha and Frida, their respective soprano and mezzo soprano voices blending seamlessly with almost chorister-style purity. Lyrically, the song refers to a brand of stage spotlight. It's a curious lyrical topic, but it works as a motif for the disaffection of touring.

ABBA's dance credentials came firmly to the fore on one track, 'Lay All Your Love On Me'. It's a powerhouse of a song, a spacious arrangement with synth stabs and a thunderous 133 bpm beat. The central synth riff is vast, and as ever with ABBA, sublime songcraft accompanies the sonic backing.

Super Trouper stands as a fine ABBA album, a work that showcases all their styles and yet stands strong as a cohesive whole. Admittedly, though, there are a few creative decisions that seem rather baffling. As a review in *The Quietus* put it back in 2011, "There are moments when melodies so infinitely, incomprehensibly sublime are married to lyrics of such incredible stupidity that you end up questioning your own sanity".

But such instances are part of ABBA's idiosyncratic charm and appeal. Over 40 years on from its release, *Super Trouper* still sounds fresh and relevant.

It's also a reminder that when it comes to creating enduring pop music, only a select few artists have ever come close to matching their achievements. ABBA are virtually without equal.

CHAPTER 4
THANK YOU FOR THE MUSIC

96 Slipping Through My Fingers

102 Discography: The Visitors

104 An Indefinite Hiatus

SLIPPING THROUGH MY FINGERS

From the top of the world to the wilderness, this is the story of the fall of a pop phenomenon

It was the late '70s, and the two golden couples of ABBA were discovering for themselves the price of fame. With 1976's all-conquering fourth album *Arrival* marking a new career peak – shot further still into the stratosphere by the 'Dancing Queen' single – the band's stock could scarcely have been higher.

But whatever stardom had given them with one hand – the platinum discs, sell-out tours, trinkets and trappings – it was taking with the other, fraying the band's sanity and fuelling an itchy paranoia. "The fans would become hysterical, banging on car doors," Agnetha told *The Daily Mail* in 2013. "Sometimes we could hardly leave our hotels. It was frightening."

No doubt, the circus awaiting the stars beyond the lobby played a part in the internal fissures now racing across the heart of the band. Under the weight of that scrutiny and an extraordinary workload – it's said ABBA only ever cancelled two shows through illness – low-level professional tensions were only natural. Agnetha admitted in that same interview that she and Anni-Frid were "very different types" – guilty of "little niggles and differences of opinion when we were a little irritated and tired of each other and of ourselves" – but never allowed these to disrupt the onstage synergy.

But as Fleetwood Mac were discovering in the same period during sessions for 1977's *Rumours* album, marriage between members of a globally successful pop band was a doomed enterprise. By January 1979, what was expected within ABBA's inner circle – and heavily hinted by the lyrical wrench of the 'Knowing Me, Knowing You' single – was suddenly and painfully public. Agnetha and Björn were to divorce after eight years of marriage, but ABBA would stride on.

"I think I wrote 'Knowing Me, Knowing You' before the divorce," said Björn in one interview. "In many ways, Agnetha and my divorce was an amicable one, we just grew apart and decided let's split up."

"We still worked very well together as musicians," he added in another interview. "So we decided to split up the marriage but not split up ABBA."

Perhaps Agnetha took it harder. In a 2008 interview with *The Evening Standard*, the singer reflected that the divorce left her "mangled" and in need of counselling, while her 1997 memoir, 'As I Am', hinted at a drama that the discreet couple kept hidden.

Opposite top: Agnetha and Björn following their divorce, 1980

Opposite right: Benny and Anni-Frid at Berns restaurant, 1979

"We always told the media it was a 'happy' divorce, which of course was a front. Obviously we all know there are no such things as happy divorces, especially when there are children involved."

Even if his marriage had run aground, Björn's assessment that ABBA still had creative gas in the tank was vindicated by the gathering success of 1977's *The Album* and 1979's *Voulez-Vous*, which both reached Number 1 in the UK and across Europe. Indeed, whether the lyrical heartbreak was dredged from the songwriter's own depths or lived vicariously through others (as he often claimed), it seemed a potent stimulant for his co-writes with Benny.

At first glance, the shining example of Björn and Agnetha's split set to song was 'The Winner Takes It All', that perfect slice of Scandi melancholy from 1980's *Super Trouper* album. But here again, the former couple couldn't agree. For his part, Björn considered the song "a fiction, because there wasn't a winner or loser in our case".

Yet Agnetha told *You Magazine* that "he wrote it about us after the breakdown of our marriage. The fact he wrote it exactly when we divorced is touching really. I didn't mind. It was fantastic to do that song because I could put in such feeling. I didn't mind sharing it with the public. It didn't feel wrong. There is so much in that song."

The dawning of a new decade did little to dispel the sense of a band peaking commercially but splintering behind the scenes. In the early weeks of 1981, it was all change, as Björn remarried to the Swedish music writer Lena Källersjö (from whom Björn divorced in February 2022). "I cried," said Agnetha. "It hurt a lot."

A month later, in February, Benny and Anni-Frid dropped their own bombshell, filing for divorce after just three years of marriage. "Actually, what has happened isn't sad at all,"

Anni-Frid countered in *Privé Magazine* that year. "We just grew apart due to different interests in life. We've always been honest to each other. We talked and talked and eventually we both came to the conclusion that a divorce was the only way out."

There was another factor, too: Benny's heart already lay elsewhere, and that November he married TV producer Mona Nörklit. "I don't know how other people deal with things like this," he told *Expressen*. "Frida and I are still friends and I'm still a member of ABBA. We are still good friends, but we are not married any more."

Despite the group's claims that ABBA functioned better without relationships to muddy the waters, listeners discerned an increasingly wistful mood on that year's *The Visitors*. This eighth album was home to both the aching breakup ballad 'One Of Us' and the slightly more pragmatic view of the bruises of an unravelling relationship explored by 'When All Is Said And Done'.

Perhaps there was something else in the air, too. Following the steady commercial upswing of the first decade, *The Visitors* hinted at a cooling of the love affair between band and public. The album still topped the chart in the UK, but the bigger picture told of withering sales, with former ABBA strongholds like France and Australia turning away.

Whispers of tension within the lineup abounded, but even now, ABBA sought to regain their mojo, repeatedly entering the studio over spring and summer of 1982, only to hit a brick wall. With a new studio album stalled, the label resorted to a hits package – *The Singles: The First Ten Years* – but it only underlined the sense of a full stop, especially when lead-off single 'The Day Before You Came' stiffed. "We might have continued for a while longer if it had been a Number 1," Björn later lamented.

That November, ABBA made their last stand on Noel Edmonds' *Late, Late Breakfast Show*, for an interview *The Guardian*'s Alexis Petridis recently described as "five of the most uncomfortable minutes of music television ever broadcast". While Edmonds probes for gossip, the four members weakly bat away rumours of an imminent split and trade passive-aggressive banter. "ABBA," writes Petridis, "visibly aren't enjoying being in ABBA very much."

They wouldn't be for much longer. For the next two years, Anni-Frid and Agnetha would insist a new ABBA album was in the pipeline, while the men suggested a career without their former better halves was unthinkable ("Who are we without our ladies? Initials of Brigitte Bardot?").

Officially, ABBA never broke up. But as a functioning unit, the band effectively ceased to exist after that final car-crash TV appearance, and when Björn was interviewed by *The Sunday Telegraph* to promote 2008's *Mamma Mia!* movie, the end seemed carved in stone.

"We will never appear on stage again," stated the songwriter firmly, then in his sixties. "There is simply no motivation to re-group. Money is not a factor and we would like people to remember us as we were. Young, exuberant, full of energy and ambition…"

Left: Back home in Sweden for Christmas, 1980

Tour rehearsals continue in Stockholm, Sweden, 1979

The group attend a royal banquet hosted by Queen Silvia and King Carl Gustaf of Sweden, 1979

THE VISITORS

ABBA's eighth studio album, the last for four decades, has been described as their Abbey Road, a bold, ambitious work created amid internal tensions

"It got frosty sometimes," said Björn of the atmosphere in Polar Studios as ABBA embarked on the recording of their eighth studio album in March 1981. It was hardly surprising. ABBA were now a band consisting of two couples who had recently separated. Björn and Agnetha had divorced in 1980, while Benny and Anni-Frid announced their divorce just weeks before recording for *The Visitors* began.

Tensions were compounded by the challenges facing engineer Michael Tretow in adjusting from analogue 24-track recording to the digital 32-track recording offered at Polar Studios in Stockholm. The first three songs had been recorded in analogue, so Tretow had to transfer all subsequent tracks from digital to analogue and then back to digital to ensure consistency of sound.

The album marked a major shift in style for ABBA, from lighter pop to a more mature and sophisticated sound. It was also darker than their previous albums. While the band's Nordic melancholy had always been cloaked in upbeat melodies, *The Visitors* focused on themes such as the Cold War, isolation and regret.

Eerie, droning synths intro the title track, which features a heavily processed vocal from Frida. Echoes of Vangelis, Kraftwerk and early Human League are in evidence. It's hypnotic, beguiling and radically different from anything ABBA had done before. It's also surprisingly catchy.

The major hit single from the album, 'One Of Us', is true to the classic ABBA sound, with lush, richly layered harmonies dominating the sound. It's a stunningly good pop song, with sparse, slightly offbeat synth bass accentuating the slow, steady groove. It's the traditional ABBA formula: an upbeat melody offsetting sad lyrics. "One of us is lonely, one of us is only / Waiting for a call / Sorry for herself, feeling stupid, feeling small / Wishing she had never left at all".

Another highlight is 'When All Is Said And Done', a poignant ballad inspired by the relationship breakdowns within the band. Piano and strings intro the track before a choral refrain sets the scene for Frida's vibrato-heavy lead vocal. "Thanks for all your generous love and thanks for all the fun / Neither you nor I'm to blame when all is said and done."

Closing track 'Like An Angel Passing Through My Room' is haunting and ethereal. Once more, Frida takes the lead

The Visitors
RELEASED 30 November 1981
TRACKLIST

SIDE A
1. The Visitors
2. Head Over Heels
3. When All Is Said And Done
4. Soldiers

SIDE B
1. I Let The Music Speak
2. One Of Us
3. Two For The Price Of One
4. Slipping Through My Fingers
5. Like An Angel Passing Through My Room

Discography: The Visitors

vocals, the lower register of her mezzo soprano bringing an ominous tone. It's a sparse, tasteful arrangement, with a ticking clock adding a sense of urgency and menace.

'Slipping Through My Fingers' centres on just how much of a child's development a busy parent can miss. The song was written by Björn after watching his daughter Linda leave the house for school one morning. "I thought, 'Now she has taken that step, she's going away – what have I missed all these years?'."

The album is not without its faults. 'Two For The Price Of One,' and 'Head Over Heels' hark back to the twee late 60s-style Europop that was sometimes evident on their early records. Benny and Björn could never resist flexing their musical theatre aspirations either, and the result is the well-crafted 'I Let The Music Speak', aptly described by Bruce Eder of *AllMusic* as sounding "like a Broadway number (and a very good one, at that) in search of a musical to be part of".

While they did not know it at the time, *The Visitors* would be ABBA's swansong, for four decades at least, until they released *Voyage* in 2021. "We might not go on working with this forever," Björn remarked in 1981. "We've emptied ourselves of everything we've got to give."

Commercially, *The Visitors* fared well, reaching Number 1 in seven countries, including Sweden, the UK and Germany. It is largely forgotten by fans but loved by the critics, regarded as an early '80s classic and an ambitious heart-on-sleeve work.

Tom Ewing of Pitchfork awarded it 8.5 out of 10 points and summed up its strength and legacy: "Even as the band's commercial star faded and its professional relationships quietly unravelled, they were perfectionists," he wrote. "*The Visitors* is not their best, but it is their most interesting [album], pointing to where Björn Ulvaeus and Benny Andersson would go next." Sadly for fans and critics, ABBA's next album was 40 years away.

AN INDEFINITE HIATUS

In 1982, the world watched in disbelief as ABBA said goodbye...

Benny and Björn at a press conference for their musical Chess, Ahoy, Rotterdam, Netherlands, 10 October 1984

If you want to know why ABBA abandoned their position as the world's premier pop artists in 1982, take a look at their final TV appearance in November that year on Noel Edmonds' *Late, Late Breakfast Show*. You can find the footage online, that is if you can bear to watch it: seated stiffly in a row, the four exhausted, irritable musicians are clearly not enjoying themselves any more.

A tired Björn, asked to pick his favourite ABBA song, reveals that the TV producers have told him to nominate 'The Winner Takes It All'. Next, Agnetha complains – accurately but bitterly – that she's "not only a sexy bottom".

As for the recently divorced Anni-Frid and Benny, when the former mentions how many great songs her ex and Björn wrote, he snaps, "Well, you never said that." In return she retorts, "Okay, so it's the first time."

None of this is fun to watch, but it does reveal why the four of them went their separate ways just weeks afterwards: they were simply sick of being ABBA. Obviously, other factors played a part: Björn once speculated, "We might have continued for a while longer if 'The Day Before You

An Indefinite Hiatus

Top: A visibly weary ABBA just six months before their split in December 1982

Right: The band released 'The Singles: The First Ten Years' in November 1982

Came' had been a Number 1". Agnetha also explained in her 2013 autobiography, *As I Am*, that her divorce from him had been stressful, saying, "We always told the media that it was a 'happy' divorce, which of course was a front. We all know there are no such things as happy divorces, especially when there are children involved."

Add a lack of creativity to the intra-band tensions and, as any musician will tell you, you have a perfect formula for disaster. As Björn told Zane Lowe of Apple Music in 2021, "We ended because we felt the energy was running out in the studio, because we didn't have as much fun in the studio as we did this time. And that's why we said, 'Let's go on a break'... We never said, 'This is it. We've split and we'll never reunite again'. We never said that. We just said back then that we'd go on a break."

Still, the idea of ABBA going on a Ross-and-Rachel style break never sat well with their audiences or their critics. The band themselves also denied it at the time, with Anni-Frid and Agnetha stating in interviews that ABBA would return for a new album. Although few people knew it at the time, the group and manager Stig Anderson had also fallen out, and in 1983 the band members sold their shares in Polar Music and walked away, apparently for good.

The fan reaction was muted, largely because no one knew what the heck was going on, but also because the four musicians embarked on other projects more or less immediately. Björn and Benny devoted themselves to a musical, *Chess*, while Anni-Frid and Agnetha began solo careers. The former kicked off her post-ABBA life with the Phil Collins-produced *Something's Going On*, the first in a sequence of successful rock albums, while Agnetha followed suit, with *Wrap Your Arms Around Me* released in '83.

It's arguable that ABBA never really went away, now we look back on this period of hiatus, because each member continued to be so productive. Still, their glory days were definitely over... or were they?

Facing the press during a trip to London, 1982

110 A 90s Revival

118 Pop Culture Pioneers

A 90s REVIVAL

ABBA's resurgence in the 1990s bridged generations of fans and ignited a sensation

The response seemed unbelievable at first. But then, it actually made sense. Why would ABBA, its powerful foursome broken up since 1982, decline an offer of $1 billion to reunite, sing those familiar songs loved the world over, and collect a mega paycheck?

At first glance, it would seem that the offer from an American-British consortium to get back together for 100 shows would be a no-brainer, even if there was some hesitation. Surely, the money was enough after an 18-year hiatus. However, it was 2000, and ABBA had already ridden a wave of renewed popularity that had begun a decade earlier. Their resurgence had proven that the glitter, the glam, the pure joy of ABBA had not faded from the scene entirely. It had just lain dormant for a while, waiting for a catalyst to ignite a fresh surge of popularity.

Then the offer came. "It's a hell of a lot of money to say no to," said Benny in an interview with the Swedish tabloid *Aftonbladet* in 2000. Benny and former bandmate Björn agreed that at least one reason for ABBA's resurgence during the 1990s was precisely the fact that the super group had not reunited. "We have never made a comeback," Björn offered. "Almost everyone else has. I think there's a message in that."

Perhaps so. Still, the bigger message, the larger implication, was simply that ABBA were too popular to pass into memory altogether. Then there is the contemplation of more excitement as evidenced by the current buzz generated with the release of new music from ABBA for the first time in four decades and the swirl of events surrounding that electrifying phenomenon.

But today's energy traces its root to the earliest era of ABBA. No doubt, it is tied to the 1990s, when moms and dads, even grandparents, fondly embraced a return of the group's spirit and its body of work after Benny, Björn, Agnetha, and Anni-Frid had shared their collective talent, personal challenges of marriage and divorce, the rigors of the road, and the triumph of their human spirit with the world.

The much ballyhooed ABBA breakup in 1982 was never formally broadcast. The band had simply seen their creative energy ebb, and along with the last days there was the realisation that a reunion might well occur – all in good time – if ever.

Right: Björn holds the Millennium Monster Award, which the group received during the 95.8 Capital FM 1999 London Awards lunch at London's Royal Lancaster Hotel

ABBA – Thank You For The Music

With over 30 million sales, 'ABBA Gold' is one of the best-selling records ever

In the breakup year, the release of the double album of ABBA's hit singles titled *The Singles: The First Ten Years*, was the group's most significant public-facing event. Two new songs failed to fully resonate, and the relative disappointment seemed to signify that the time had come to part ways. Benny and Björn worked on the musical *Chess*, while Anni-Frid and Agnetha looked to their solo careers.

While the mid-1980s may be described as the doldrums, or simply a period in the shadows, by the early 1990s an awakening occurred. ABBA and their mystique came back with renewed vitality, but the surge was not due directly to any particular effort by the band members themselves. Many observers point to the release of the four-track extended play cover of jewels from ABBA's formidable catalogue by the pop duo Erasure. Their offering, titled *Abba-esque*, skyrocketed to the top of the charts across Europe.

When U2 came to Stockholm for a June 1992 concert, the acknowledgement of ABBA's star power was throttling up. Bono and company brought Benny and Björn to the stage for a rousing reboot of 'Dancing Queen'. The signature song once again became familiar fare on the European radio waves, peaking at Number 16 in the UK.

In September, the compilation *ABBA Gold: Greatest Hits* took the market by storm, sales of 31 million making it the best-selling album in the band's history. 5.5 million sold in the UK alone, making it the second-highest-selling

A 90s Revival

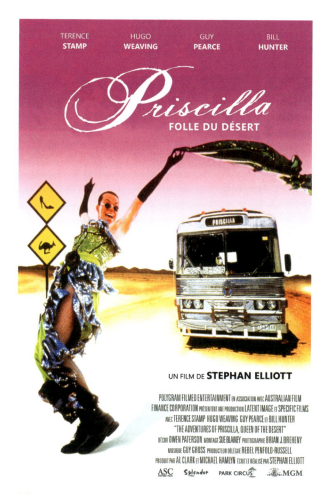

A French poster for 'Priscilla Queen of the Desert'

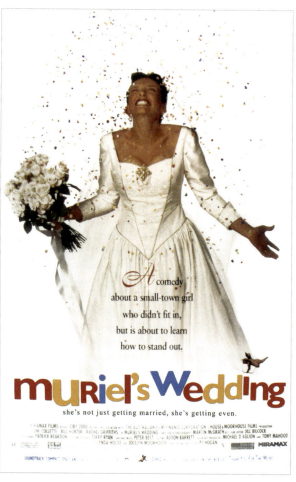

A 'Muriel's Wedding' movie poster featuring Toni Collette

album in the nation's history, trailing behind only Queen's *Greatest Hits*, which boasts over 6 million UK sales to date.

What could be better? Well, more. *More ABBA Gold: More ABBA Hits* reached store shelves in 1993 and generated even more excitement, with 3 million sales. The 1994 boxset *Thank You For The Music*, a four-disc tour de force including all the great hit songs, other selected tracks and even some rare and previously unreleased recordings was perfectly timed and brought all four ABBA members together during its compilation. At the same time, tribute bands and variety acts brought more attention to the ABBA mystique – perhaps generating curiosity at first but then turning a new generation onto the group's unique lyrical, rhythmic and pure pop presence.

Left: Popular tribute group Björn Again performing in July 1999

In 1994, ABBA's songs were featured on the big screen. This time, however, the vehicle was not a presentation of concert footage. Two feature films that live on as cult classics emerged that year. Director Stephan Elliott brought *The Adventures of Priscilla, Queen of the Desert*, forward, while director P.J. Hogan developed the box office smash *Muriel's Wedding*. Both movies showcased familiar ABBA hits. As Muriel's favorite band, ABBA provides a thread of continuity throughout the latter, and of course, it seems fitting that the setting for both films is Australia, where the super group's popularity had always remained vibrant.

Benny and Björn allowed the filmmakers to use ABBA's music only two weeks before *Muriel's Wedding* entered production, and the result was a stunning success. The film grossed $57.5 million at the box office, and 'Dancing Queen', 'Waterloo', 'Fernando' and 'Mamma Mia' were

An ABBA themed float takes part in the annual Brighton Pride Parade

back on the radio, as well as the lips of listeners, both 'old' and new. Incidentally, *The Adventures of Priscilla, Queen of the Desert* was also a box-office success, grossing $29.7 million on a budget of a mere $2 million.

By the end of the 1990s, ABBA had reached new heights of popularity. The musical *Mamma Mia!* premiered on London's West End in 1999, and the Broadway opening followed two years later. When the show made its Stockholm debut in 2005, it was only the second occasion to bring all four ABBA members together since 1986. *Mamma Mia!* became a worldwide sensation, seen by more than 60 million people in 440 cities across the globe. Its Broadway run concluded in 2015, making *Mamma Mia!* the ninth-longest running show in the history of the Great White Way. The 2008 feature film spawned by the musical starred Meryl Streep, Pierce Brosnan, Colin Firth, Amanda Seyfried, and Christine Baranski. It's box office take topped $615 million and generated a sequel.

To date, the ABBA phenomenon has spanned more than half a century. Through the triumph and the turmoil, a solid fanbase has stayed steady and, in fact, grown. Among those most loyal fans, band members have given a nod of thanks to the gay community around the world. From the glitzy early performances through the troubling depths of the AIDS epidemic and into the 21st century, the gay fanbase has proven stalwart.

Björn was blunt in his assessment of the gay community's initial and lasting loyalty. In 2011, he appeared at an event honoring ABBA sponsored by the Swedish gay magazine *QX*. "In the '80s, ABBA was distinctly uncool, totally out," he admitted. "And I thought, 'Well, this was it. It was fun as long as it lasted but now it's over.' But in some strange way we still remained popular in the gay scene. And, maybe it sounds like I'm buttering up, but I don't care. When we got a revival in the 80s, early 90s, I'm sure it's because we still were popular in the gay scene."

Fans queue outside the Cadillac Winter Garden Theatre in New York City to watch the production

Indeed, ABBA members have made appearances at gay pride celebrations through the years. In 2013, Agnetha told OUT magazine that the essence of ABBA's magnetism resonated with the gay community. "I think it partly comes from how ABBA was presented from the start – with high heels, spectacular costumes and music you wanted to dance to."

Since the beginning, the broad appeal of ABBA, its staying power and its blend of upbeat pop tempered with real, human emotion has resounded worldwide. To be sure, ABBA will remain a force in the entertainment industry. Witness its past, revel in its present, and anticipate its future!

Manager, songwriter and friend Stig Anderson, pictured here 1986, passed away in 1997

British actor Colin Firth stars alongside America's Amanda Seyfried in the 2008 blockbuster movie 'Mamma Mia!'

POP CULTURE PIONEERS

Even in their absence, ABBA still managed to rule the world

The great paradox of ABBA is that in their absence, they got bigger. Can you think of a band as in demand as ABBA were between 1982 and 2019 – even though they existed only as a brand?

Proof of the foursome's continued appreciation by the public and, perhaps more significantly, by the bankers and fund managers behind the music industry, came in 2000. Around this time, a rumour – unproven, but still persuasive – circulated that ABBA had been offered a billion US dollars to perform a reunion tour consisting of 100 concerts. That's 10 million bucks per gig, which adds up to a conservative 1 to 2 million dollars for each member for a single show, even after the taxman has taken his cut.

To put that into perspective, a mid-sized band will net that same 1 to 2 million dollars across a reasonably successful tour, not just a single gig. And yet ABBA turned it down. Money just wasn't a motivator any more: they each had plenty of that. If ABBA were going to return to the stage, a simple string of performances wouldn't be enough to get them back into the old silver spandex.

With all of that understood, we did in fact see Björn, Benny,

Left: Benny and Björn holding their Special International Awards, which they received during the 2002 Ivor Novello Awards in London

Agnetha and Anni-Frid together in person, laughing and chatting like they'd never been away, in 2008 and 2018, before the current reformation was ever heard of. These reunions took place at the premieres of their two blockbusting films, *Mamma Mia!* and its sequel *Mamma Mia! Here We Go Again*, which ABBA accurately regarded as far more culturally impactful than any mere sequence of live shows.

The movies were also just the latest manifestation of a behind-the-scenes ABBA industry that had never really gone away. Although most of us know that the movies were a success – the first film in particular took $615 million at the box office, an astounding 12 times return on its modest $50-million budget – their real ongoing cultural impact has come from the original *Mamma Mia!* stage play, which has been playing more or less constantly everywhere since 1999. In dozens of cities around the world, from the West End to China, theatres have been resounding with ABBA songs to theatre-goers for two decades, putting the brief cinematic run of the movies in perspective.

Why would ABBA take that billion-dollar offer to perform an exhausting world tour, when billions were already flowing in from the play and the movies? Not to mention the income from the film soundtracks, which finally gained them the American success they'd never enjoyed before: in August 2008, the *Mamma Mia!* soundtrack topped the Billboard charts, becoming ABBA's first-ever Number 1 in the U.S. The band didn't even need to write any new music for this release.

Note, too, that ABBA's music was being re-recorded and re-released more or less constantly by the time that lucrative offer was made in 2000. Sure, there had been a fallow period for the band for a few years after the start of their hiatus in 1982: in the early to mid-'80s, pop fans were all listening to Duran Duran, Simple Minds and Tiffany, and ABBA seemed a touch old-fashioned.

Yet as the years passed and the wheel of fashion kept turning, we found ourselves returning to the earworm melodies and luscious vocals of those old hits – and by 1990, suddenly those songs didn't sound old any more. They sounded irresistible.

The first evidence that new bands were turning to ABBA for inspiration came in 1992, when the synth-pop duo Erasure released a covers EP called *Abba-esque*. A British chart-topper, the impact of the EP was such that the long-running Australian ABBA tribute band Björn Again released an answer record called *Erasure-ish*, with two Erasure songs recorded in an ABBA style.

In 1994, two Australian movies both centred on ABBA's music – *The Adventures of Priscilla, Queen of the Desert* and *Muriel's Wedding*. Both of these were cool, cult films that didn't break any box-office records, but that was actually better for ABBA than if they'd been blockbusters,

Pop Culture Pioneers

Barry and Robin Gibb of the Bee Gees with Ann-Frid and Benny onstage at the 25th Annual Rock and Roll Hall of Fame Induction Ceremony at Waldorf Astoria, New York, 2010

positioning the music among an educated elite. For the first time, ABBA's music was popular among alternative audiences who generally despised mainstream culture.

What the original ABBA members made of all this is not known, but we like to think they found it amusing – and perhaps a little inspirational. They certainly didn't object to other artists covering their songs, with Björn and Benny guesting on stage with U2, then the biggest rock band in the world by some distance, at the Irish band's Stockholm show in '92. 'Rock' is the operative word in that sentence: ABBA's music had long since transcended musical genre boundaries, with musicians from the soul, blues, grunge and metal worlds professing their love for the songs.

For evidence, take a look at the range of ABBA cover versions that have been released over the years. Just some

Left: Theatre owner Sir Cameron Mackintosh, Camilla Parker-Bowles, Björn, Anni-Frid, HRH Prince Charles and producer Judy Craymer photographed at the Royal Charity Gala Performance for the musical 'Mamma Mia!' at the Prince of Wales Theatre in London, 2004

of these include Sinéad O'Connor's take on 'Chiquitita', prog-rock experimentalist Steven Wilson's version of 'The Day Before You Came', a grunged-up cover by the Lemonheads of 'Knowing Me, Knowing You', Cliff Richard's 'Lay All Your Love On Me', and two very different versions of 'SOS' by soul singer Dionne Warwick and the bizarre British comedian Frank Sidebottom. Even the Swedish heavy metal guitarist Yngwie Malmsteen paid tribute to his countrymen with a version of 'Gimme! Gimme! Gimme! (A Man After Midnight)'.

It seems that musicians love covering the songs as much as the rest of us love listening to them. From 1998 to 2004 there was a Swedish pop band, the ABBA Teens, later renamed the A-Teens, whose schtick was to record ABBA songs in a 1990s style, an inspired idea that led to serious sales figures. Several compilations of ABBA covers exist, variously titled *ABBA: A Tribute*, *Abbasalutely*, *ABBAmania* and so on. The singer Cher, who appeared in the *Mamma Mia!* movie, actually released *Dancing Queen*, an entire album of ABBA covers, in 2018.

The four members attend the opening of Mamma Mia! The Party, a restaurant in Stockholm where people can eat while watching a show based on ABBA's songs, January 2016

As a result of all this activity, by the mid-2000s ABBA were a serious commercial entity again. In the semi-final of the Eurovision Song Contest 2004, broadcast from Istanbul 30 years after ABBA had won it with 'Waterloo', all four members appeared as puppets in a film called *Our Last Video Ever*. The following year, 'Waterloo' was voted the best song in Eurovision's history, a verdict that is difficult to disagree with. Also in '05, Madonna sampled 'Gimme! Gimme! Gimme! (A Man After Midnight)' in a single called 'Hung Up', which supposedly topped the charts in over 50 countries. Can you imagine the revenue from that song in the pre-Spotify era?

By 2010, the brand was literally everywhere – in a *SingStar ABBA* game for the Sony Playstation; winning a PRS poll in which the British public voted for ABBA as the band they would most like to re-form; and even in a political controversy.

The latter occurred when the right-wing Danish People's Party used 'Mamma Mia' at rallies, causing an aggrieved ABBA to launch a protest: however, Universal Music had

The entrance to the ABBA Museum

Part of the recording room at the ABBA museum

already agreed the song's use by the DPP, and no further action was taken.

In London, a 25-room exhibition called ABBAworld was launched, featuring interactive activities; a similar, but permanent, venue called ABBA The Museum opened in Stockholm. "You can get up on stage with ABBA avatars and become the fifth member of ABBA!" says the museum's website, whose slogan "Walk In. Dance Out" is actually pretty effective. You'd visit it, wouldn't you?

And yet a full-on ABBA reunion always seemed unlikely.

A man plays a piano at an advertising hoarding outside of the ABBA museum, Stockholm, Sweden, May 2013

Natalie Abbott, the new Muriel, attends a preview event for 'Muriel's Wedding The Musical' in Melbourne, Australia, 8 October 2018

Sure, there was the odd hint that something might happen in due course – for example, when they all appeared at an event called Mamma Mia! The Party in Stockholm in 2016. Their British manager Simon Fuller announced the same year that they would be working on a new 'digital entertainment experience' to launch in the spring of 2019. Yet it still didn't feel like a full-on coming-together.

Even the arrival of ABBA's music on TikTok in the summer of 2021, while welcomed by excited fans, still didn't generate the same buzz as the idea of actually seeing the band performing on stage again, digitally or otherwise. It seemed that a real reunion could never happen. After all, the band had said as much throughout the years since 1982. If only someone could conjure an idea to convince them to take a chance…

CHAPTER 6
A NEW VOYAGE

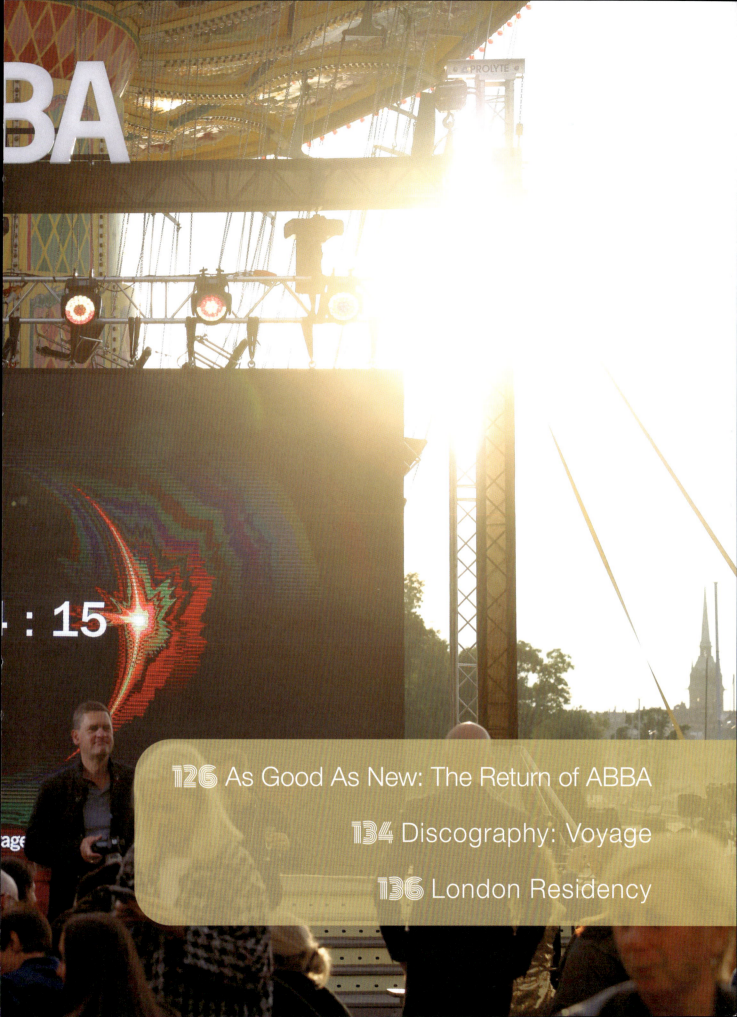

126 As Good As New: The Return of ABBA

134 Discography: Voyage

136 London Residency

AS GOOD AS NEW: THE RETURN OF ABBA

It seemed nothing could tempt ABBA back from the wilderness. But after a shock reunion, a torrent of new tunes and the birth of their digital doppelgängers, here we go again…

One billion dollars. For most pop bands, the figure reportedly dangled over ABBA's bank accounts at the turn of the millennium would be an offer they could hardly refuse. So it was some measure of the group's resolve to never again tread the same stage that what could have been the biggest fee-per-show tour in history was turned down flat. "It was never put on paper," said Björn in *The Guardian*. "But then, everyone knew we wouldn't do it."

As the first decade of the millennium unfolded – bringing with it the gargantuan success of the *Mamma Mia!* jukebox musical and $615-million-grossing movie – it seemed that while ABBA's stock had never been higher, there was no carrot that could lure the Swedes back into the spotlight.

The family ties between the two former couples meant the members still met at intervals, far from the paparazzi's lens. But to anyone outside of ABBA's fiercely guarded inner circle, the band were pop's most invisible superstars. Unseen. Unheard. Almost glacial in their anonymity.

The story went that Agnetha was living in the wilds of Sweden, burnt by fame and done with the circus. "I didn't sing at all for 13 years," she told an ABBA biographer in a rare interview. "I didn't even have a hi-fi at home. I never wanted to play another record again."

As for Anni-Frid, she had been visited by family tragedy since ABBA closed for business and was likewise living off the radar in Switzerland. Benny could sometimes be spotted in the streets of Stockholm, en route to the studio where he would tinker with music that seemed destined never to be heard. Only Björn maintained anything like a profile, continuing to twinkle for journalists in his role as ABBA's representative on Earth.

Right: ABBA on the big screen during their Voyage event at Gröna Lund (an amusement park in Stockholm) on 2 September 2021 showcasing their first new song after nearly four decades

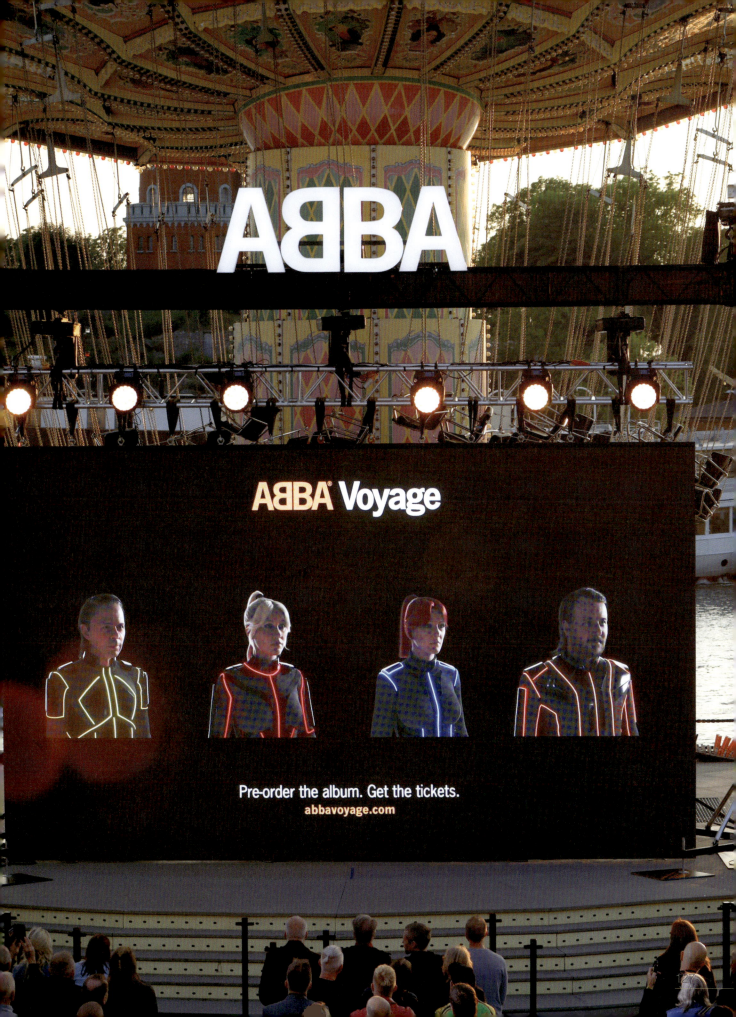

Björn in his studio on Skeppsholmen in Stockholm, Sweden, 20 October 2011

The man who started the thaw was Simon Fuller. As the brain behind *Pop Idol* and manager of the Spice Girls, the British entrepreneur was a wily operator of the music business's machinery. Critically, too, Fuller recognised what other suitors had not: that any approach requiring ABBA to tour (always the band's least-loved duty) was doomed to failure. "Simon came and he had an idea," Benny told Alexis Petridis. "We can go on the road but we didn't have to be there ourselves."

The whispers became official in October 2016: the four members of ABBA were working on "an extraordinary new virtual-reality experience". Even then, Fuller's deal faltered, the band's enthusiasm cooled by plans to render them as holograms and march them onto the promotional treadmill with miscellaneous TV specials.

But before reaching that impasse, ABBA's creative wheels had begun turning once again. At first, Björn and Benny hoped to present just one or two new songs on the mooted tour, perhaps as a show of continued creative strength, rather than accept their status as a greatest-hits act. As Björn told *The Telegraph* in 2008, "I remember Robert Plant saying Led Zeppelin were a cover band now because they cover all their own stuff. I think that hit the nail on the head…"

But when their heads came together, the dormant partnership surged into high gear, with those few songs snowballing into the spine of a miracle ninth album. Sessions were swiftly booked at Stockholm's Riksmixningsverket studio with Agnetha and Anni-Frid, and with the glow of the red light came the glorious discovery that even after decades of inactivity, both women still had voices that could bring down the angels.

Meanwhile, writing 'trend-blind' was a calculated risk, with all concerned agreed that if the new material didn't match the vintage hits of *ABBA Gold*, the whole enterprise would be scrapped. Yet the revelation was that the new songs taking form were ABBA in excelsis, from the wistful swoop of 'I Still Have Faith In You' to the rebooted disco of 'Don't Shut Me Down'.

Both were logical choices for a double-A-sided single, leading out the *Voyage* album that arrived in November 2021 to scale both the charts you would expect (Number 1 in the UK, Australia and across Europe) and those you wouldn't (Number 2 on the U.S. Billboard). "All these years after 'Waterloo'," Rob Sheffield wrote in *Rolling Stone*, "ABBA still refuse to surrender."

Even now, the flesh-and-blood ABBA remain elusive. A condition of the band's reunion, revealed the menfolk to *The Guardian*, was that Agnetha and Anni-Frid could duck press duties. As for live performances – the real money-spinner – the band were plotting a giant leap that would give fans the experience of an ABBA concert without the schlep across the planet.

Although Fuller had discovered the hard way that a hologram concert was a non-starter, perhaps there was another way. The band sought out the George Lucas-founded Industrial Light & Magic for the SFX wizardry that would birth the much-heralded 'ABBAtars'. With Björn previously telling reporters that a fatal barrier to any reunion was the thought of a decrepit ABBA, this was the solution: a quartet of digitally de-aged avatars representing the band in their '70s prime, with stage moves bottled by motion-capture suits and a phalanx of 160 cameras. Wearing these 'mocap' suits, the band worked through every song in the set list: a painstaking process that took five weeks.

"The technology has given us the ability to do this, but the important part is the music," director Baillie Walsh stressed to *Dazed*. "We're not going back to the past and recreating a '70s concert – this is what ABBA would be doing now if they were young and on tour."

ABBA Mania get ready for their West End return outside Waterloo station, 14 May 2021

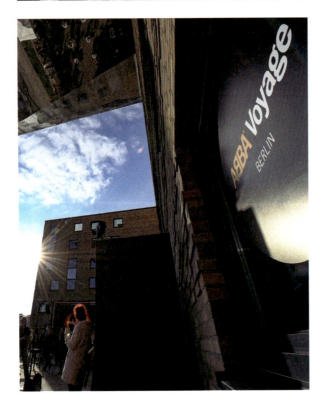

The performances of ABBA themselves were to be pre-recorded, but the ten-piece orchestra that accompanied their vocals each night would play in real-time and perfect synchronicity. "I had to go through my mental memory bank of musicians I'd played with," said ex-Klaxons keys man James Righton to *NME* of the task of corralling this live band. "I've been making music for quite some time now, so I know a lot of musicians who'd be able to play this music. I had to put the feelers out very tentatively and confidentially for people who'd be up for the task of being in ABBA's band."

At a time when so much as setting foot on a stage was outlawed, the Voyage concept represented the boldest live brief since the supersized stage designs of the '70s. And while the sheer infrastructure of transplanting the tour from city to city ultimately proved unworkable, the band hit on a winning compromise, putting down roots at a dedicated space in London's Queen Elizabeth Olympic Park and letting the people come to them.

The Voyage concerts began in May. The more slippery question is when they will end. Agnetha insists that ABBA is done. Anni-Frid prefers "never say never". Benny says "this is it" – but his observation in *The Guardian* that "the stars of the show will never tire" raises an interesting theory. Could the Voyage shows become a residency without end, playing ad infinitum to a new busload of tourists each day, and theoretically outliving the four members themselves?

As Björn remains fond of reminding us, ABBA never strictly ended in 1982. Perhaps it never will…

Top left: Commercially savvy as ever, ABBA have stepped into the face mask market

Middle left: Jan Sport and Michael Musto perform onstage during the ABBA Voyage event at Rumsey Playfield, Central Park, New York City

Left: Fans and press wait outside the nhow Hotel in Berlin, Germany, for the ABBA event ABBA Voyage to commence

Right: Zoe Ball poses with Björn and Benny during the London launch of ABBA Voyage, 2 September 2021

As Good As New: The Return of ABBA

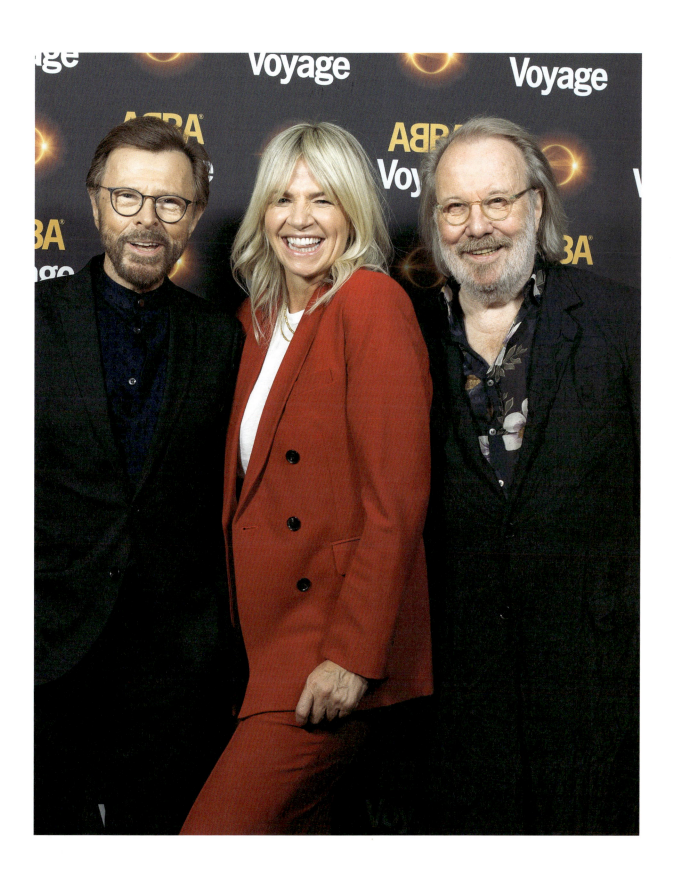

ABBA's first album in four decades, 'Voyage', hits shelves in Berlin, Germany, 5 November 2021

ABBA – Thank You For The Music

VOYAGE

After a gap of 40 years, ABBA have regrouped for an album of mixed sonic offerings that has yielded two stunningly good singles

Four decades on from the album that seemed certain to be their last, ABBA returned with a hugely anticipated release that was met with equal measures of joy and derision. It's fair to say that ABBA only realised how popular they were once they'd split up back in 1982.

By the '90s, their back catalogue was being reappraised by 'serious' music fans and musicians who acknowledged, with no irony, what an exceptional and unique band ABBA were.

Over the decades, they turned down numerous offers to reform. In 2017, Benny told the Swedish newspaper Expressen that there were plans to tour 'virtually'. In April the following year, the four members issued a statement saying that they had recorded two new songs, 'I Still Have Faith In You' and 'Don't Shut Me Down'.

Then, on 2 September 2021, a globally screened press conference in London confirmed that a new album, *Voyage*, would be released on 5 November, with a series of virtual concerts taking place in London from 27 May 2022. The album would feature ten tracks, including the two already recorded, while the concerts would feature a live band playing alongside the band's avatars.

The opening ballad on the album is 'I Still Have Faith In You'. It's the first of two big singles, and it soars. Strings intro the track before Frida's resonant mezzo soprano voice enters the mix, sounding as warm as ever but deeper, age having enriched the textural nuances of its timbre.

The song has the quality of a musical, which is not surprising given Benny and Björn's colossal post-ABBA success with the musical *Chess*. It's poignant and beautiful and seems to acknowledge the weight of emotion from across the decades. "I still have faith in you / It stands above / The crazy things we did / It all comes down to love".

'Don't Shut Me Down', the other major single on the album, features a lead vocal from Agnetha, which is equally as rich as Frida's. There's a sparsity to the instrumentation on the opening section, with epic, flowing strings underpinning the plaintive vocal. At 0:38 the drums and bass kick in and suddenly it feels like classic ABBA, with Agnetha and Anni-Frid's vocals in flawless harmony against a brisk and buoyant backing

Voyage
RELEASED 5 November 2021
TRACKLIST

SIDE A
1. I Still Have Faith In You
2. When You Danced With Me
3. Little Things
4. Don't Shut Me Down
5. Just A Notion

SIDE B
1. I Can Be That Woman
2. Keep An Eye On Dan
3. Bumblebee
4. No Doubt About It
5. Ode To Freedom

track. Lyrically there are telling moments: "I have learned to cope, and love and hope is why I am here now".

The breakdown of both couples' relationships in ABBA has been compared to those in Fleetwood Mac. The big difference, though, is that neither Agnetha or Anni-Frid wrote the songs, so any lyrics about breaking up come solely from Björn and Benny's viewpoints. It all feels somewhat skewed, as the *NME* noted in its review of *Voyage*: "There is a slight element of wish fulfilment, perhaps, in Ulvaeus and Andersson writing lyrics like 'but he is a good man' for their ex-wives to sing."

'No Doubt About It' falls somewhere between whimsical late '60s Europop and a stage musical and recounts the experience of having a row with your partner. "I made a mess this time / And there's no doubt about it / Hands down, the fault is mine / And I'm prepared to shout it". 'Just A Notion' meanwhile is another light, danceable track with rolling boogie-woogie piano and brass stabs.

'When You Danced With Me' offers a sprightly sonic contrast, with its use of uilleann pipes and references to Kilkenny. There's a real simplicity and charm to the track and the sparse roots feel reflects Agnetha and Anni-Frid's '60s folk roots.

The wonderfully plaintive piano intro of 'Little Things' rapidly segues into a Christmas song, and from then on there's a teetering balance between heartfelt honesty and festive schmaltz that plays out to the bitter end. In a similar vein, 'Fernando'-like flutes pervade the childlike 'Bumblebee', which almost descends into parody. That said, every ABBA album had its kitsch moments and that was part of what endeared us to them.

Voyage is not a great album and it's hard to see what it actually achieves. It does induce a warm nostalgia in the listener and exudes a kind of purity, containing as it does impeccable performances, sublime moments and majestic production, as well as some frankly addled lyrics. It's certainly worthy of a place in their illustrious back catalogue.

Even so, it's doubtful that this album is worthy of bookending such a unique and stunning musical legacy. Still, who's to say that this will be ABBA's final studio album?

ABBA – Thank You For The Music

LONDON RESIDENCY

London Residency

In 1977, few would have imagined that ABBA would be playing in London in 2022

An aerial view of the Queen Elizabeth Olympic Park, where the London Tour dates are held

Like their music, which has always been composed and engineered with the utmost precision, the smooth, ultra-professional way in which ABBA managed their rebirth as a live band in 2022 has been nothing less than astounding. When they announced a run of part-live, part-digital shows in London dubbed ABBA Voyage, starting on 27 May 2022, it was obvious that every single part of the puzzle had been fully realised and long in the planning.

First, the most important part of the shows, the four digital avatars – the 'ABBAtars' – haven't just been created by some random animation studio. The virtual Björn, Benny, Agnetha and Anni-Frid were painstakingly made by none other than George Lucas' Industrial Light & Magic (ILM), one of the world's state-of-the-art CGI companies. The four musicians, now in their seventies, strapped themselves into skin-tight jumpsuits and performed dance moves choreographed by Wayne McGregor, resident artist at London's Royal Ballet, for a production team that included *Chernobyl* director Johan Renck, former David Bowie videographer Svana Gisla, and Benny's son Ludwig. It was later revealed that body doubles were used to help get the singers' trim 1977 physiques back, and that Björn and Benny even shaved off their beards to enable the facial digitisation.

"They got on a stage in front of 160 cameras and almost as many [digital] artists and performed every song in this show to perfection, capturing every mannerism, every emotion, the soul of their beings – so that becomes the great magic of this endeavour. It is not four people pretending to be ABBA: it is actually them," explained Ludwig.

In addition, the choice of venue was perfect. The shows are held in a pop-up venue, the 3000-seater ABBA Arena, at the Queen Elizabeth Olympic Park in London – and of course, if the event had to happen at all, it had to be in the UK, ABBA's spiritual home… and most lucrative market. As

ABBA avatar tickets go on sale in London

London Residency

Fans of all ages are turning out to enjoy the show

Andersson diplomatically put it: "London is the best city to be in. When it comes to entertainment – theatre, musicals, concerts – it is all here... There is a big audience travelling here for that reason. It was a no-brainer." Björn added, "We have always felt the Brits see us as their own", which is, of course, quite true.

It's thought that the idea of using singing avatars backed with live musicians originated with Elvis: The Concert in the 1990s, when the late Elvis appeared in video clips accompanied by a band. He even 'ad-libbed' jokes between songs. Talking of the live band, ABBA – or their 1977 selves – perform with a ten-piece band put together by Klaxons guitarist James Righton.

After opening to critical and popular acclaim in May 2022, Abba Voyage, which features 10 new songs (from the album of the same name) as well as all the band's biggest hits, has gone from strength to strength. Described as "ground-breaking" and "needs to be seen to be believed" it's still packing in the fans week after week. Originally scheduled to finish in October 2022, dates have now been released up to May 2023, and there is no reason why the avatar-driven tour shouldn't run and run. "The seven shows-a-week VR experience could run for years. The arena can be broken down and transported across the world," speculated *iNews*, and who are we to disagree?

Watch this space. The story isn't over yet.

" I'VE LEARNED NEVER TO SAY NEVER. YOU JUST DON'T KNOW. I ENJOY SINGING. I STILL SING – AT HOME "

ANNI-FRID LYNGSTAD
WHEN ASKED ABOUT A POTENTIAL COMEBACK IN 2014